China

THROUGH A GLASS OF WINE

by Noel Shu

CHINA
THROUGH A GLASS OF WINE

by
Noel Shu

Copyright Page

@Copyright 2016 Noel Shu

ISBN 978-1-63393-012-4

All rights reserved. No portion of this publication may be reproduced or utilized in any form or by any means, electronic or mechanical, including photocopying, without permission in writing from the publisher.

Published By:

Café con Leche

Table of Contents

Introduction - CHINA'S WINE INDUSTRY	7
Chapter 1 - GOVERNMENT ANTI-CORRUPTION CAMPAIGN	15
The Chinese Love of Wine	17
Domestic Wine Production	20
The Song of the Grape, by Liu Yuxi	22
Domestic Wine Culture	27
Foreign Wines in China	31
Sparkling Wine	35
Chapter 2 - HISTORY OF WINE IN CHINA	38
Traditional Forms of Chinese Wines and Spirits	40
Early European Style Wine Influence in China	41
The People's Republic of China Promotes Red Wine	44
Foreign Investors Expand Wine Production in China	45
France's Influence on China's Winemaking	47
China's Wine Market	50
Chapter 3 - Current and Cultural Landscape	56
E-commerce	58
Wine Education and Marketing	60
Tradeshows and Events	63
Wine Distributors	66
Bars and Restaurants	68
Guidelines for Exporting Wine to China	69
Chapter 4 - FAKE WINE	83
Police Destroy Fake Wine in China	89
Chapter 5 - THE CHATEAUS OF CHINA	109
Hansen Winery	109
Helan Qingxue Winery	116
Chateau Changyu Moser XV	121
CONCLUSION	125
CITATIONS	128

CHINA
THROUGH A GLASS OF WINE

Introduction

CHINA'S WINE INDUSTRY

*M*y father was one of the first guys to own a motorcycle in Beijing. I have it on good authority that for a while there, only he and the Mayor, Mr. Xie Fuzhi, had one. Fuzhi was military and they have been riding around on those things since the '30s. I can just imagine the feeling: Long Soviet-style avenues, a few domestically manufactured cars idly turning, and my dad barreling down the street at 60 miles per hour on a Huanghe motorcycle. To be on a motorcycle in Beijing must have been like owning a Pegasus in the Middle Ages. They had complete and irrefutable freedom and precision; gliding past fruit vendors, ox-carts, rickshaws, and clumps of olive-clad soldiers returning from training in their stained uniforms.

"Freedom" is better sensed than explained and it has been an elusive concept for me, my dad, and perhaps the majority of my countrymen. Now that we're here, what exactly do we do? We live in a world where China has become the largest consumer of luxury goods, sucking down cognac, Rolexes, and BMWs in the bottomless hearth of the world's second largest economy. Our Confucian values are competing with the ever-increasing rate of change, the skyscrapers are materializing overnight on the Pearl River Delta, and the buzz of fiber optic cables is humming through the entire nation.

As I write this, I'm sitting at home in a glass and brick house on Long Island. On my desk, there's a laptop and a bottle of wine next to a pile of family photographs. I put my hand on the label. Trust me, that part becomes important later. A photo of my parents is on top of the pile. "Linda" is my mom's American name. You know, in China we get to pick our own Western names, right? We typically pick those that are easy to pronounce with nice, hard, double or triple syllables that we reconstruct in the tonality of our language. "Lin-Da" almost sounds like Chinese if you hit the last vowel hard enough.

Just like my mom, Dad also had an easy Western name, Leo. His story of what he accomplished after immigrating to the United States is truly a remarkable one. Coming to the United States as a college student, he was part of the first group approved by China. Upon arriving, he was carrying a ticket stub that signified he was actually the seventh person to legally travel to the United States after the Mao administration. During his earlier years, he spent his time in Tennessee working with a team tasked to complete the "Genome Project."

My parents met sometime during the 1980s in Boston. They then went on to start their own import-export auto engines and parts company. My parents had the advantage of sourcing auto engines and parts from China and selling them in the States at a very competitive price. If companies in the States wanted to do business with China, they ultimately had to turn to my parents. They saw their company exponentially grow and dominate within only a few short years because they got into the auto industry when there was a high demand and a short supply for low- priced auto parts.

At some point in this equation, I was introduced.

They say bi-cultural kids are neither truly of one culture or the other. It emanated from China before I was even born that I could never be Chinese because of the cultural disconnect. And of course, I could never be American either. I would always be "Chinese-American." My Mandarin was good, but rudimentary at times. I was able to communicate well with others and even had a Northern accent on occasion in my Chinese which sometimes became an interesting topic of discussion.

The main reason behind this is that Beijing-accented Chinese is considered the most mainstream and standard form of Mandarin. Having a father from Beijing and a mother from Shenyang, I ended up inherently speaking with both of their natural accents in my Chinese. People in China view me merely as an American with an Asian complexion. It is impressive when an American speaks fluent Chinese and a winning combo when an American speaks Chinese with both an authentic Northern U.S. and Beijing accent.

Me AKA the Author

It turned out that the key to unlocking my past was China's voracious new hunger for all things foreign. A new generation of Chinese has risen, known as the "tuhao" – which loosely translated means, "tacky rich" or "nouveau riche." These are the new rich who buy priceless art, vintage wine, stock their entire wardrobe with luxury brands, and generally lack the manners or sophistication to go along with their accumulated wealth. Social media networks on the mainland abound with photos of young men and women in designer eye-glasses, pounding giant bottles of Dom Pérignon, crashing their Lamborghinis, vacationing in Monaco, and being arrogant to the chagrin of the general population.

This new usage of the term "tuhao" first went viral after a joke appeared on the Chinese social platform, Weibo, in 2013. It went like this: a wealthy but unhappy young man asks a Buddhist monk for advice. When the monk holds out his hand, the young man is perplexed and says, "Master, are you telling me that I should be thankful and give back?" To his surprise, the monk replies, "Tuhao, let's be friends!" The joke implied that the tuhao's wealth even made a monk greedy.

The tuhao's greed is contagious and the government has been determined to put a stop to it. Over the last few years, the tuhao have made enough of a stir on social media that their very presence was deemed to be a threat by the government. A crackdown was initiated on "conspicuous consumption," or the practice of "blinging and bragging." Golf, expensive wines, Rolexes, and Ferraris were all on the black list as grounds for imprisonment, fines, or worse. From gold iPhones to gold-wrapped Bentleys with Gucci seats, those who were deemed to unfairly gather wealth were now in the government's crosshairs. Over 70 of these billionaire kids were even sent to a social responsibility school where they were taught manners and how to behave in a way that would not embarrass their parents or their government.

That see-saw between power and humility would come to define much of my life. As far back as I can remember, we were always well off. I recall going to Catholic school in Queens when my parents bought the Mercedes G-500 the first day it was available. The huge, boxy vehicle with its military design was fitting for my family because daily life was often about grades and extracurricular activities such as piano, kick-boxing, break dancing, sports, and virtually anything that would have a long lasting and positive impact.

I was a good natured kid from what I recall, sheltered, but amiable. In schoolyard politics, I was a nomad. I would hang out with the band kids one day and hold my own with the jocks the next. At around age eight, I hit a growth spurt that left me tall and somewhat invincible in the social pecking order; or at least it deflected any bully's ambitions by turning me into a seemingly "hard target." Those years whizzed by as they do and I saw my parents give birth to two more baby boys, my brothers, and—in accordance to Chinese culture—my charges.

No one ever expected, least of all me, that this road would pave the way to a bottle of cabernet sauvignon and a passion for all things wine: especially Chinese wine.

It is extremely difficult to find Chinese wine outside of China. New York City, which carries pretty much anything you can hope to find, is almost dry when it comes to wine from China. Its large wine distributors, high-end wine shops, and tony Asian restaurants will all give you a blank look if you ask for imported Chinese wine. In fact, here's a secret: pretty much the only nook where you'll find a few bottles is down an alley lined with fishmongers and incense shops in a place called Yoshi Wine and Liquor. Even here, they only carry two brands—Chefoo, a red wine owned by the Chinese wine conglomerate Changyu, and Kuei Hua Chen Chiew, a dessert wine made by Beijing's Dragon Seal Wines. They're both around five dollars and guess what? They taste more like you got them for two dollars.

I will provide you with a play-by-play on how China is about to be known for producing quality wine, just like Napa and Sonoma became globally accepted as producers of quality wine a generation ago, and Australia a decade ago. If critics are any indication, China could soon be on the cusp of being home to the next Yellow Tail. In describing a vintage 1998 Great Wall Cabernet, the Wall Street Journal said, "Real wine — deep-colored, full-bodied, tannic, but with a lot of fruit — that could have held its own with cabernets from other countries." Sticker price? —$72 a bottle in Shanghai.

Let's explore that $72 bottle of the decent cabernet. You see, even though there are a few dozen producers in China making decent wine such as this one, their retail prices are still relatively high — and frankly, the value is not quite there yet by international standards. Most of China's high-end producers are mom-and-pop operations that simply don't have the scale of competing wineries in Australia, Europe, or the United States. As you continue your wine journey through China you will learn what kind of effect the high retail prices have had on China's domestic wine producers.

Chapter 1

GOVERNMENT ANTI-CORRUPTION CAMPAIGN

The days of endless streams of '82 Lafite uncorked at the banquet table — the Chinese equivalent of a boardroom meeting happening over a lazy Susan in a smoky VIP room at a snazzy restaurant — are over. That move, however, has given the domestic market perhaps the biggest push yet. Interestingly, the intersection of wine and great power has never been more blurred in China. In fact, the very geopolitics of China's ascent — and now austerity — can be traced back to those hefty bottles of reds.

The story begins in November 2012 when Chairman Hu Jintao began the political transition of handing the reins of the world's largest economy over to former vice-president Xi Jinping. Of course, events had already been set in motion by March of that same year when a massive corruption scandal involving former Communist Party chief Bo Xilai erupted in the headlines. It didn't help that there was a spicy side story involving the titillating murder of English businessman Neil Heywood by Bo Xilai's wife.

The unprecedented scrutiny of political corruption at all levels of government directly led to the tightening of excesses and the austerity measures that were shortly announced afterwards by the new president, Xi Jinping. Indeed, one of his first proclamations was to clean house. He specifically prohibited alcohol consumption and gift giving by party cadres. In 2013, some 182,000 officials had been punished for corruption, "extravagance," and abuse of power. The timing couldn't have been more apropos, coming right before the Chinese New Year which is the biggest cash cow for wine producers that supply a lot of entertaining and gift giving.

The rest is history. Wine imports went from 50-70% year-on-year growth to less than 5% in 2013. Between 2006 and 2012, the number of companies importing wine to China had leaped from 800 to more than 5,000. It's made somewhat of a recovery to date but even still, the massive slump has opened room for the domestic production market to sneak in a toehold.

In most of China's history, political campaigns have ebbed and flowed with many taking their course and then disappearing as soon as they appeared. But there's no sign this anti-corruption campaign is going away any time soon. In fact, in 2014, the crackdown heightened even more with tens of thousands of officials arrested. Among the litany of restrictions has been a ban on all extraneous meetings and "empty speeches." Prior to this, there was a culture of all sorts of conferences on essentially useless action plans used merely as a pretense to get inebriated on extravagant wines. The impact of this crackdown can't be understated, and it's not just on the expensive wines.

Indeed, the austerity campaign wasn't just an effort to put an end to the indulgent party cadres swilling down '82 Lafite, but it encompassed all levels of government as well. Government spending on banquets has fallen by over 50%, while some 50 hotels had to be downgraded from 5 to 4 stars just so they could attract government business (thereby creating a loophole for officials to do business there since 5 star hotels are now officially banned).

According to Bruno Paumard, a renowned French winemaker who is currently working with Château Hansen in Ningxia, wine sales in China fell by as much as 50% that year. Specifically, between 2012 and 2013, Changyu's sales declined by 23%, Dynasty Fine Wines was down 18%, and China Foods (the beverage division of COFCO which heads up China's largest wine brand, Great Wall) saw a whopping 52% drop. Despite the government crackdown, e-commerce has led the way to avoid the stigmas of excess to satiate the burgeoning taste buds of the middle class.

The Chinese Love of Wine

According to the 2013 figures compiled by the London-based company International Wine and Spirit Research, China's wine drinkers consumed a staggering 1.86 billion bottles, or 155 million nine-liter cases of vin rouge (red wine), out-drinking both historical powerhouses France and Italy; 150 million cases and 141 million cases respectively. This has been an increase of 136% over five years, making China the leading market for red wine. The Chinese annual average consumption of red wine is only 1.5 liters per person.

But why all the enthusiasm for wine? The most interesting thing to note is China's love of wine may be associated with being "Western" and therefore exotic. Ever since social media giant Facebook was banned in 2009 after the riots in Xinjiang, but subsequently reinstated in Shanghai's twenty-eight kilometer "free trade zone" in 2013, China has been showing signs of detente, embracing certain elements of globalization—albeit cautiously. As with social media, so follows the ripple effect of exposure to common Western customs, conviviality with wine being among one of those. One can assume that as the barriers decrease, consumption can only increase.

There is a strong correlation between the rise of the middle class and the nouveau riche of China, otherwise known as the yuppie culture. No longer content with the ways of their forebears, the young Chinese are branching out into new realms of exotic experience with their new-found wealth and snatching up luxury items such as wine as a symbol of their independence. According to award-winning author Helen H. Wang, much like the folkloric American Dream, young Chinese are chasing after their own version of collective optimism; the Chinese Dream, if you will. In fact, nearly 800 million Chinese are considered part of the middle class—that's more than the entire population of the United States.

Another similarity to the American Dream is the subsequent Chinese version of appearing well off to your friends and neighbors, or the syndrome known as "keeping up with the Jones'." Wang remarks that "... Chinese are status conscious people. They would pay premium prices for products and services that can enhance their 'status.' But for products and services that their neighbors and friends cannot see, they would be very price conscious. For example, the woman who bought Gucci shoes might not spend more money on first class airfare.[1]"

Wine—especially expensive wine—is seen as a lavish expense, commonly shared with others, which is a common practice in modern China. In contrast to Western cultures, wine is often offered as a toast in Chinese culture, being consumed in its entirety after making magnanimous gestures towards prosperity. Of course, there is a gradual shift towards the Western traditions of meal pairings, low-key wine tastings at nightclubs, and casual consumption among youth culture. The inherent refinement of wine, along with its subtle qualities, makes it a perfect fit in modern Chinese culture. And, just like any other country, let's

---

1   Wang, Helen H. (December 5, 2011). *My Speech at Asia House in London*. Thehelenwang.com. Available from http://thehelenwang.com/2011/12/my-speech-at-asia-house-in-london/.

not forget the traditional sophisticated air that newly-minted aficionados feel at quaffing the beverage.

Tied in with the status of wine may be something as simple as symbolism. In China, red is traditionally the color of the Communist government. Because business is often lubricated over a few glasses of pinot that is synonymous with power, luck, and wealth, it can have a subconscious effect on sealing partnerships. White wine's unpopularity has a lot to do with the marketing and perception of the people of China today. There is even a minority that believes white wine is associated with the color of death, which is white.

I feel that white wine is actually what the Chinese prefer—they just don't know it yet. It is the most easily accepted wine because it has a slight sweet note and is less strong and overwhelming. Most of the wine education in China concerns red wine. Therefore, it is up to the industry professionals to better educate the Chinese people about white wine. However, with the Chinese market maturing and becoming more knowledgeable about wine, white wine is gaining a newfound preference among savvy consumers.

Domestic Wine Production

According to the International Organization of Vine and Wine, China has become the second largest vineyard area in the world after Spain in 2014, with China having about 800,000 hectares of land devoted to vineyards. However, it is important to note that only a very small percentage of China's vineyards are devoted to growing grapes for wine production. The majority of grapes grown in China are used for table grapes and raisins. Even with France falling to third place in vineyard area, it still led the world by producing 46.7 million hectoliters of wine. Italy followed with 44.7 million hectoliters while Spain made the top three with 41.6 million hectoliters of wine. China with its vast vineyard area only managed to produce 11.1 hectoliters of wine.

What's not commonly known is that China's wine production isn't a modern phenomenon, but dates back more than 4,600 years. In 1995, an archaeology team consisting of American archaeologists and members of the Archaeology Research Institute of Shandong University investigated two sites twenty kilometers northeast of Rizhao. They discovered the remnants of a variety of alcoholic beverages. These included traditional Chinese alcoholic beverages such as rice wine, mead (honey wine) and most notably, grape wine. Out of more than two hundred ceramic pots discovered, seven were used for the production of grape wine and the remains of grape seeds were also found.

Between 130 and 120 BC, the Han dynasty began diplomatic relations with a number of Central Asian kingdoms. Many of these kingdoms produced grape wine. The end of the second century BC saw Han envoys bringing grape seeds from the kingdom of Dayuan to China and planting them near the capital city of Chang'an (present day Xi'an in Shaanxi Province). Throughout the following centuries the grapes were grown, perhaps most notably in northwestern Gansu. They were not used to produce wine on a large scale, however, and remained an exotic domestic product known only by a few people. Several poets even wrote verses, including Liu Yuxi (772 – 842) from the Tang Dynasty who commemorated wine's unique attributes towards status and wealth in "The Song of the Grape."

The Song of the Grape, by Liu Yuxi

We men of Tsin [Jin = Shanxi], such grapes so fair,
Do cultivate as gems most rare;
Of these delicious wine we make,
For which men ne'er their thirst can slake.
Take but a measure of this wine,
And Liang-chow's [Liangzhou's] rule is surely thine.[2]

However, to fully understand China's modern domestic wine industry of mass production, one must look back over a century ago during the tail end of the Qing dynasty. Established in Yantai, a coastal city located in the province of Shandong, Changyu Winery began its first large-scale production of wine in 1892 under the direction of the politician and businessman Zhang Bishi. It is the country's oldest and largest winery. To this day, the Shandong province remains the leading producer of wine, growing 40% of China's wine grapes. Two decades later, in 1910, French friars

---

2   Sampson 1869, p. 52. Cited in Shafer 1963, p. 145.

started the Beijing Winery (now known as Dragon Seal Wines), producing wine used in the ceremonies of Chinese Christians.

The Author at China's "first" winery (Changyu)

Since then, foreign funding has emerged with the loosening of restrictions of the '80s and has thrived despite the austerity. The Great Wall Wine Company began with imported equipment from Italy, Germany, and France in 1979. One year later, the French company now known as Remy Cointreau, created Dynasty Wines through their investment in Tianjin. French ingenuity and capital aided Dynasty in establishing European-style best practices and, as a result, is recognized as a producer of quality Chinese wines.

Changya Pioneer Wine, Great Wall Wine and Dynasty Fine Wines Group are often called the "Big Three" of Chinese wine. They own a majority of the country's wineries with combined revenues estimated at $8 billion, according to a 2015 article from International Business Times (IBT)[3]. So why is it that China's "Big Three" wine producers have not even made a dent in the international market when wines from smaller producers like Chile and South Africa can be found in many cities throughout the world? Michael Wu, Vice-Chairman of the Chengdu-based Chinese Wine Associates Alliance (CWAA), said in an email to China Daily, "The Big Three want to go to the US, but they don't really have the capability now. In other words, they want to go to any market that would accept them. Considering our population of 1.4 billion, I don't think they have an impulse to export to the US now.[4]"

There may be some reluctance on the part of the domestic Chinese producers to expand into the U.S. markets. For now, China seems content to export to nearby Macau and Hong Kong. Combined with existing austerity measures and decreased production, Wu may have a valid point. Domestic wine producers can barely keep up with the demand of the Chinese people as it is. This might explain why it is so difficult for an American wine connoisseur to find a bottle of Dynasty

---

3   Florcruz, Michelle (May 03, 2015). *China's Wine Industry Explodes, But Not Yet On The World Stage*. IBTimes.com. Available from http://www.ibtimes.com/chinas-wine-industry-explodes-not-yet-world-stage-1902284.

4   Freifelder, Jack and Jibu, Bian (October 30, 2015). *Wine in the US: 'Made in China' is rare*. Chinadaily.com. Available from http://usa.chinadaily.com.cn/2015-10/30/content_22325719.htm.

or Great Wall wine on any American store shelf. It is an interesting conundrum. There are domestic shelves to stock before producers even consider crossing oceans.

Though this booming market may seem like the ideal place for Chinese vintners to build muscle for future international endeavors, the situation is not without its pitfalls. With the focus on quantity, the quality of domestic wines has the risk of faltering. The high-end boutique operations are not what we are talking about here. These specialty producers have the quality but they lack the quantity and therefore they lack the ability to be competitive internationally. The focus is on the larger producers that actually have the potential and scale to reach foreign markets. China "will need a few flagship brands to be able to compete at the high end," says Karl Storchmann[5], an economist at New York University and editor of the Journal of Wine Economics. There are trends to be found in the stories of other foreign wine markets that have gone through similar transitions in their quest to find the balance between quantity and quality.

---

5   Florcruz, Michelle (May 03, 2015). *China's Wine Industry Explodes, But Not Yet On The World Stage*. IBTimes.com. Available from http://www.ibtimes.com/chinas-wine-industry-explodes-not-yet-world-stage-1902284.

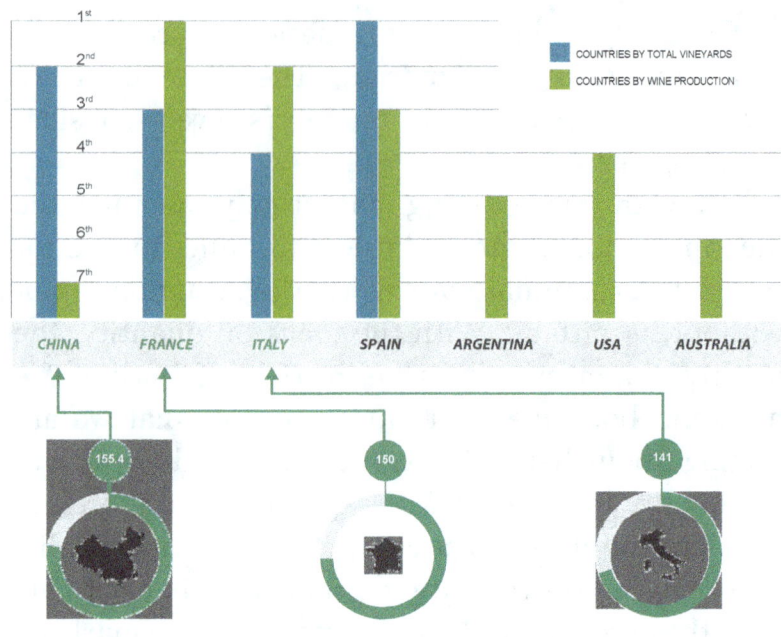

Domestic Wine Culture

While domestic production may have decreased due to government restrictions, China's embrace of wine culture has spread to extensive holdings abroad. In the famed wine growing region of Bordeaux, Chinese holdings have increased from 2% to a whopping 25% between 2009 and 2012. Chinese businesses own more than sixty vineyards and have become the largest source of foreign investment in the region. The advantage is twofold: circumventing the government's stifling austerity restrictions and opening up instantaneous access to distribute to the lucrative Chinese market.

Domestically, a number of wineries and chateaux have been spreading to the wine growing regions, such as the popular Ningxia region, with all the amenities normally associated with famed regions like Napa. There are even street signs shaped like wine bottles. There is no shortage of famous vineyards to explore in the Ningxia region and no expense has been spared when it comes to creating an atmosphere that is impressive to tourists.

For example, Chateau Changyu Moser XV Vineyard is lit up with colorful lights for a nighttime show and inside there are exhibits to display the finer points of how their wine interacts with the taster's palette. Moët Hennessy's Domaine Chandon Ningxia Vineyard is vast and outfitted with stunning, modern dining rooms and other amenities for visitors. Other major wineries include Chateau Lilan Winery, Chateau Lanny Winery and Resort, XiXiaKing Chateau Yuquan Winery, and several others that are in the planning and construction stages.

There are many famous wine growing regions in China besides Ningxia. The Yunnan, for example, is in the Southwest and has earned the nickname of "Asia's answer to Bordeaux." This region has been dominated by domestic ice wine makers Shangri-La and Sun Spirit since the early 2000s. Their products are mediocre at best and aimed solely at the domestic market. But French luxury wine producer Moët Hennessy and Australian producer Cape Mentelle have recently invested in the Yunnan province in order to produce cabernet sauvignon, merlot, and cabernet franc grapes.

The tides are turning in the Yunnan province and very soon the region will be known globally for producing quality wine. The hotels and resorts are certainly on the way. The Golden Pebble Wine Resort may be indicative of the coming change, with foreign investors bringing modern wine culture into China to take advantage of the country's massive potential of producing and serving quality wine that will gain the respect of both the domestic and international wine critics.

The Golden Pebble will be situated in of the city of Dalian at the tip of the Liaodong peninsula. It will include a full production winery, a hotel, a commercial village, and residential villas. According to Bruce Write, the vice president and principal architect, "China's exploding wine market has been well-documented, but the country's winemaking culture in the modern era is still in its infancy. With the Golden Pebble Winery Resort, we have the unique opportunity to help define what the culture of winemaking looks and feels like in China, particularly on the Liaodong Peninsula. This will be the first winery in the Liaoning province, and we are honored to be designing all elements of the winery and resort.[6]" There is already a Golden Pebble beach resort in Liaodong and the region is known for its beaches, golf, and temperate climate. It seems that the location is primed for one of China's first wine resorts with the promise of additional wine resorts that will open in Ningxia.

The many unique variations of climate in China have provided a challenge in some regions that have led to creative solutions. The coastal regions are mild and offer traditional growing operations that mimic the wine-growing regions of the west. However, some of the wine country is located at the foothills of mountains near the Kazakhstan border in the north-west which makes use of the climate there a major endeavor. In these challenging areas, winters are extremely cold and the grape vines need to be buried in order to keep them alive.

There is a unique aspect that is born from such harsh environments; ice wine. Grapes are allowed to freeze on the vine which results in a sweeter product that normally is associated with esoteric regions like

---

6   Hebert, Heather (July 21, 2014). *Winery Design in China – Defining China's Wine-Making Culture*. Sb-architects.com. Available from http://www.sb-architects.com/winery-design-defining-chinas-winemaking-culture/.

Hungary. The UK Retailer Barry Bros. & Rudd is the first UK retailer to distribute Chinese ice wine and other wines outside of the domestic market. This provides an opportunity to the international wine taster to experience some of the more mature Chinese wines available. Ripe avenues like this can put China on the map for encompassing their staggering potential.

Of course, the infrastructure for large-scale production and luxury consumption is in place for China's apparent world domination, but there can be no better indication of what's really going on than taking a look at the smaller players on the burgeoning wine scene, namely wine bars. Despite the government austerity and social stigmas associated with wealth, wine bars are booming. Take as an example Dr. Wine, Shanghai's "favorite wine bar" that features two stories of conviviality, catering to sharply dressed twenty and thirty-somethings. Not to be outdone, there's Roosevelt's Wine Cellar, boasting not only the largest wine cellar in Shanghai, but in the world. In Beijing, there's Bordeauxthéque, boasting one of the most specialized collections of Bordeaux-based wines in the city, if not the entire country. Smaller wine bars without large-scale ambitions certainly proliferate throughout the city, creating the impression that there's simply no difference between China and the rest of the world. If you uncork it, people will come.

Despite the promise of China's wine regions being set for tremendous growth, there are still obstacles to overcome as the young industry learns and grows. The reviews of tasters have been all over the charts, but most will agree that China is on the right track with wine and has all the skills, tools, and land needed to produce internationally competitive wines with unique character. The momentum is powerful in China and it seems for certain that the Chinese wine industry will—pun intended—finish strong.

Foreign Wines in China

The wine action in China is not all domestic. International wine producers are competing fiercely to get a piece of the Chinese market. Tmall.com, one of many online storefronts for the Alibaba Group, has recently begun to connect Chinese wine consumers with American wines such as Robert Mondavi cabernet sauvignon; a wine owned by Constellation Brands, Inc. Constellation Brands is among the first of the wineries to be featured in Tmall.com's, "Tmall Vineyard Direct" e-commerce site. The demand of Chinese consumers is simply too great for domestic producers to keep up and foreign producers are happy to step up to the plate to meet that demand and fill the wine void. American wines have been taking a backseat to imports from France, Chile, South Africa, Australia, and others, but now American wineries such as Twin Oaks and Woodbridge will be available as middle shelf options in a slowing Chinese economy.

Of course, Chile and South Africa were themselves small wine producers at one time. Presently, Chile and South Africa are locales that are equated with quality wine, but it was not always that way. For years, the South African wine market was dominated by the Co-operative Winegrowers Association of South Africa, or KWWV. This co-op ensured that farmers would be compensated for their wine, but it also favored quantity over quality and bad practices were implemented for years that resulted in the production of a prolific amount of low quality wine.

On top of that debacle, Apartheid was in effect. Anti-Apartheid trade sanctions meant that international markets were unavailable to South African vintners. Fortunately, Apartheid was dismantled in 1994 along with the KWWV, clearing the path for a free market that would inspire the competitive development of quality wines and open the door to international trade. Boutique wineries sprouted up all across the country and, suddenly, South Africa was on the map again. Exports exploded after such a long isolation from the international market. The world wanted the unique experience of a South African wine.

The Chilean Wine Industry suffered in similar ways during WWII when heavy taxes were implemented and social policies designed to limit alcohol consumption were put into effect. The following years of political unrest continued to keep the wine industry in shambles. The industry was still geared towards production of cheap wine to satisfy a struggling populace and not equipped to focus on producing wines of a finer quality for the international market. With the return of democracy in 1990, things started to look up again and Chile became another success story much like South

Africa. The doors opened to international investors and buyers lined up to revitalize the scene. Today, it is easy to find quality Chilean wine at your local store.

The fact that China is the world's biggest market for red wine has inspired foreign wine producers to move rapidly by investing in the Chinese wine market. In 2011, France's Domaines de Rothschild (DBR), producer of the renowned Château Lafite, planted its first vines in China, mainly cabernet sauvignon grapes, with an initial 37 acres in Penglai, a hilly peninsula on the east coast of Shandong providence with a century-long history of winemaking. DBR described its first 2013 Chinese vintage as "experimental" and expects to reach perfect maturation for its 2016 vintage. At that point, only if they are satisfied with the quality, would they allow the world to taste Chinese "grand crus."

In 2011, Moët Hennessy, the wine and spirits arm of France's LVMH luxury group, embarked on a new venture in China to produce and sell high-end sparkling wine under its Chandon label. Its first Chinese vineyard is 163 acres, located in the Ningxia Hui Autonomous Region in the northern part of the country. This area is ideal for growing chardonnay and pinot noir grapes. For the first time in 2012, Moët Hennessy went into producing high quality red wine in China, investing in 74 acres in Southwest China's Yunnan province. It will grow mostly cabernet sauvignon and merlot grapes. The Bordeaux style blend will be labeled Au Yun and will be sold at a premium price.

The French connection with their big investments in China's wine market has raised the Chinese consumer interest in domestic wine. The urban, hip Chinese are very brand conscious and, just like their lavish taste in cars and clothing, their taste in wine is almost certainly centered on prestige labels like Château Lafite Rothschild, one of the five quintessential producers of Bordeaux.

It isn't difficult to see how the history of wine in Chile and South Africa correlates with the present condition of the Chinese wine industry. All of these countries have spent time in economic isolation and have been prevented from exporting and importing wines with the rest of the world. They have been discouraged from producing and consuming alcohol via taxes and social policies. Yet, despite this, their domestic populations have a strong passion for wine and the international community has a great interest in their potential. If the development of the Chinese wine industry continues along this path, it can be expected to become quite the international competitor in the coming years as its domestic industry is given the chance to flourish and refine itself. International investments have been made and everyone is watching and waiting.

Wines from the United States are starting to gain a foothold in China and the numbers are surging every year. However, this does not mean they have a firm grasp of the Chinese wine market. Many Chinese are starting to broaden their horizons of New World wine and that is precisely why there is a double-digit increase in U.S. imports every year. However, the Chinese are still very much inclined towards French wine which is their go-to wine. If they do not know what to bring or buy for an event, they play it safe and buy wine from France. Consequently, wines imported from the U.S. to China make up a small percentage of the market share while the French own the lion's share of Hong Kong's foreign wine market.

A majority of the wine exported to China from the United States comes from Napa County, California. Napa has the reputation for producing the best wine in the U.S. and the Chinese are not just drinking wine produced in Napa, they are also buying vineyards there. With California at or near the top of the spectrum of quality wine, it's not hard to see how it will continue to grow its market share in China.

In China there is a general lack of awareness that other parts of the U.S. produce quality wine because other countries such as France, Italy, Chile, Argentina, and Spain are aggressively marketing their wine in China. The USDA Foreign Agricultural Service put out a report in 2013 called *South China's Hidden Treasures Report* which points out how crucial it is for American regional wine associations to visit South China's emerging second and third tier cities which are flourishing and have strong purchasing power. The smaller tier cities offer a tremendous opportunity for the U.S. wine market which will be growing at a faster pace than the first tier city markets.

Sparkling Wine

Champagne, France was the original source of sparkling wine and is considered the most famous wine region in the world. Its wine is associated with both luxury and celebrations, or just kicking back and enjoying with the special people in your life. Besides France, many other countries around the world produce sparkling wine including Italy, Spain, Australia, Chile, South Africa, the United States, and the United Kingdom. Recently, China began producing sparkling wine, particularly in the Ningxia Region where the French Champagne maker Moët Hennessy has taken root in producing sparkling wine.

Only sparkling wine that is produced in the Champagne region of France can be truly called "Champagne" and holds the reputation of producing the very best bubbly because of its own unique system of classification. France organizes wine with the Appellation d'Origine Contrôlée (AOC) system which links a product with its geographical origin and has rules that apply to nearly every aspect of wine production. Some of these rules include approved grape varieties, vineyard planting density, method of pruning, and aging requirements. These regulations protect the reputation of the Champagne wine producing part of France that resulted in very strong brand awareness. Whenever someone chooses sparkling wine from Champagne, there was no mistake that they are drinking sparkling wine of the highest quality.

The large Champagne Houses (Maisons) buy their grapes from many grape growers all over the region. They are the large Champagne brands, or negociants, that we are familiar with, such as Moët, Mumm, Perrier, and Veuve Clicquot. They have a lot of purchasing power which enables them to get the best grapes from the best growers, producing a consistent taste every year. Maisons can be identified by the initials NV (Non Vintage).

On the other side of the market is Grower Champagne, which is more terroir focused. The estate that owns the vineyards around the village within the Champagne region produces the wine. Since their grapes are grown on specific plots of land, their Champagne would taste very different each year. A Grower Champagne is identifiable by the initials of RM (Récoltant Manipulant) present on the wine label. Grower Champagne is a recent term that has become increasingly popular among consumers.

The Chinese sparkling wine market continues to grow even though some analysts think that Chinese people only prefer red wine. As mentioned earlier, there are already regions in China growing grapes to produce sparkling wine. Even with some obstacles to overcome, the sparkling wine imports to China from countries such as Italy, Spain, and France have been growing steadily over the years. The rising incomes and changing tastes of the Chinese middle class are creating quality and status conscious consumers that are looking to escape tradition and familiar tastes. Sparkling wine is very untraditional in China and has a huge growth opportunity that will continue to increase as the industry raises awareness by educating the Chinese people on this particular wine category.

Chapter 2

HISTORY OF WINE IN CHINA

The consumption of wine in China dates back at least 5,000 years.

"Although wine drinking is a common cultural heritage enjoyed by various peoples world-wide, the wine drinking culture of each people is different. The origins of fermenting and drinking wine in China go far back in time. The Chinese either used wine as a libation to their forefathers to express reverence, or enjoyed it by themselves while writing poetry or prose, or to toast their relatives and friends during a feast. Without a doubt, wine occupies an important place in the culture and life of the Chinese people. Wine was intimately connected with most Chinese men of letters. It was also an inseparable part of the life of ordinary Chinese people. It was a must for the banquets of ancient emperors and kings. Every sort of wine vessel thus became an important kind of sacrificial object."

— Pieter Eijkhoff, Wine in China

Then there are the old folktales like "Tu Kang Makes Wine" about a mythological figure in China who is also referred to as the "God of Wine." Legend has it that he invented wine over two-thousand years ago.

Perhaps most special of all Chinese wine culture heritages is the poetry written in dedication to wine by Li Po (701 – 762) from the Tang Dynasty and translated into English by various authors, including this translation, by Arthur Waley.

Drinking Alone by Moonlight - by Li Po

A cup of wine, under the flowering trees;
I drink alone, for no friend is near.
Raising my cup I beckon the bright moon,
For he, with my shadow, will make three men.

The moon, alas, is no drinker of wine;
Listless, my shadow creeps about at my side.
Yet with the moon as friend and the shadow as slave
I must make merry before the Spring is spent.

To the songs I sing the moon flickers her beams;
In the dance I weave my shadow tangles and break.
While we were sober, three shared the fun;
Now we are drunk, each goes his way.
May we long share our odd, inanimate feast,
And meet at last on the Cloudy River of the sky.

Traditional Forms of Chinese Wines and Spirits

The two most traditional forms of wine consumed by Chinese over hundreds of generations are "plum wine" and "rice wine." Plum wine, still widely sold and consumed today, has a very sweet taste. Rice wine is actually close in taste to Japanese sake (Japanese learned how to make it by borrowing recipes from the Chinese). It can also remind one of homemade vodka made out of wheat or potatoes. Rice wine bottles often contain dead lizards, dead bees, and pickled snakes. The belief is that, while terrifying to the public, creatures inside the rice wine bottles would provide a powerful tonic effect to the consumer. In order to avoid confusion when ordering European white wine in China, remember to say that you are ordering a Chardonnay or Sauvignon Blanc. Otherwise, you might get a bottle of rice wine with a pickled snake in the bottle.

In addition to these two types of wines, the national drink of China that has been around for thousands of years is baijiu, which translates to "white alcohol" or "white spirits." It is a distilled alcohol between 80 and 120 proof made from sorghum and other grains. Baijiu is usually enjoyed in China during holidays, business meetings, or any occasion involving a group of men. While it is a drink typically consumed by men, women are known to partake in drinking baijiu from time to time. To the Western palette, baijiu is reminiscent of rubbing alcohol or diesel fuel.

Chinese specialists on the history of grape wines (putaojiu) in China insist Chinese knew how to make wine out of grapes since the dawn of their civilization, namely since the Zhou Dynasty (1122-221 B.C.E.). Although there are reliable proofs that grapes were known to Chinese since this relatively early period, it is undeniable that when grapes were subjected to fermentation, they were subjected to the same "ferment cake" technique that was used for making grain wines. Furthermore, the end product was not intended for direct consumption, but resulted in wine used for cooking.

Early European Style Wine Influence in China

Introduction of European-style wines designed for direct consumption with meals is undoubtedly related to the spread of Catholicism in China. The first import of wines from Europe happened during the Ming Dynasty (1368-1644) when Spanish and Portuguese traders found their way to South China and established missions there.

Based on the available records, Catholic missionary priests began arriving in China during the 13th century. Italian Franciscan priest, John of Montecorvino, arrived in Beijing (Khanbalik) in 1294 and, in just five years, built the first church. He built the second church in 1305 close to the Imperial Palace. From what we know, the Roman Catholic Church's religious rituals were fully observed in both churches that he established. In order for the Catholic ritual of communion to be properly executed, red wine must have been used in the Eucharist symbolizing blood of the Savior, Jesus Christ.

Then, during the Ming Dynasty (1368-1644), Matteo Ricci established a permanent Catholic mission in China, further spreading the knowledge of European wines and also elevating the status of red wine in particular. To this day, Yunnan remains one place where traditional European wine-making lasted uninterrupted for nearly 100 years, starting from the vineyards planted by the Catholic missions of the 19th century. "Yunnan Rouhong" and "Shangri-La" are two distinct wines related to this time period.

One of the earliest documented accounts of European-style grape wine in China dates back to 1892. Zhang Bishi, an officer of the Qing government, traveled back to China from Europe and introduced European vinifera grape varieties to the Chinese people. The lush, undulating hills and mild climate in summer provided the perfect place for planting grapes in Yantai, Shandong province. Employing an Austrian consul as his winemaker, Bishi founded the Changyu Winemaking Company, which is now known as Changyu Pioneer Wine Company, China's oldest and largest wine producer. Around the same time Zhang was establishing the European vinifera varieties, the Germans built the Qingdao winery and the French established Shang Yi (which went on to become today's Beijing winery).

Beijing Dragon Seal, one of China's earliest popular European-style wineries, was founded in 1910 by a French clergyman, Shen Yunpu, who set up a vineyard near Heishanhu Church. He converted the church's graveyard into a wine cave and hired a French oenologist to produce both red and white wines for church use only. By 1912, the winery was also producing sparkling wine. Shangyi School took over their production in 1933 and made wines under a new label, Chala. In 1946, the winery grew in popularity and some wine was even exported to Europe. In 1959, it was officially named the Beijing Winery by the government and soon became a renowned producer and market leader.

It was during the 1920s and '30s that grape wine drinking gained popularity in China. European-style wine became more popular in the early 20th century, but was still not as popular as rice and plum wines. People from Hong Kong to Shanghai to Macau began drinking it as a more refined, less strong alternative to baijiu or strong distilled spirit wines. Grape wine was considered rare and therefore became a pastime of the wealthy.

Around this time, the idea of grape wine consumption started to gain traction and the early entrepreneurs who grasped this novel idea were among the first to reap its rewards. However, there was still a very long road to travel before most of China could enjoy a glass of red wine as easily as they could enjoy plum wine or distilled spirits. This takes us to the next monumental change in the Chinese political system and social structure which allowed the use of European-style wine to spread across the country.

The People's Republic of China Promotes Red Wine

Mao Zedong was the founding father of the People's Republic of China that was established in 1949 due to the culmination of over two decades of civil and international wars. He remains a controversial figure over his legacy both in China and abroad. Unfortunately, his policies caused the deaths of tens of millions of people in China. His supporters credit him for unifying China and ending decades of civil war, and claim that his policies laid the foundation for China's rise to an economic super power.

After the 1949 revolution, the Chinese government paid a lot of attention to grape growing and wine production. Under government supervision, wine was promoted and made from grapes and other fruit in order to reduce the use of grains that went into making spirits. This happened throughout Northern China. The five leading provinces that saw the expansion of land devoted to grapes were Xinjian, Hebei, Shandong, Liaoning, and Henan. Two-thirds of all the grapes in China were produced in these provinces.

During that time, China did not allow outside cultural influences. This resulted in a limited advancement of wine-making due to its lack of modern wine production technology it could have acquired from foreign countries. That all changed under the leadership of Deng Xiaoping in 1978 when the Chinese government began to pursue an open door policy in which it looked to achieve economic growth through the introduction of foreign capital and technology.

This produced the greatest revolutionary shift and expansion in China's wine production.

By the mid 1990s, the Chinese government was trying to spread the word to its citizens that they had no reason to fear the return of the great famine during Mao's reign. The solution was to reduce using grains to distill spirits because this grain was vital to feed the growing population. To offset this waste of grain that was needed to produce food, Premier Li Peng criticized the negative impact of grain spirits on people's health and marveled about the benefits of red wine in his 1996 presentation to the People's Congress. This sent a signal to everyone that red wine was approved by the Communist leadership.

Foreign Investors Expand Wine Production in China

In 1980, Dynasty became the first winery with foreign investors to form a joint venture between Remy Martin and the Tianjin Agricultural Bureau. Then, in 1982, distiller Seagram established Great Wall Winery in Shacheng located in the Hebei province. They used modern techniques to make their wine with technology brought in from foreign countries. What they produced at first was table wine. In 1985, Huadong was China's first "chateau-style" estate to plant and produce varietal and vintage-dated wines with an appellation, Tsingtao, on the label. A British wine merchant from Hong Kong established this label in Qingdao.

By that time, China's economic output was four times what it was in 1979 and this coupled with the "red explosion" in the international wine market in the early 2000s meant large increases in production for Chinese wine. Millions of liters of red wine were also put on the market for bottling in local wineries. Companies that distilled spirits shifted their factories over to wine production.[7]

Small-scale wineries and bottling companies exploded into existence across the nation. Over 100 new wineries opened between 1996 and 2004. Large-scale wineries set up chateau-style showcases with surrounding vineyards, offering the opportunity for wine tourism just like their Western counterparts. Grace Vineyards of Shanxi province and Bodega Langes in Hebei are solid examples of beautiful chateau wineries that are open to visits from the public.[8]

Europe and America are watching rapid Chinese expansion carefully with the Europeans especially keen to become an integral part of the trend. Among France's most famous vineyards, Chateau Lafite is one of the most eager foreign wine producers to partner with the Chinese government for investment in the Shangdong Peninsula, commonly known as the "Bordeaux of China." Chateau Lafite's owners, the Rothschilds, made an announcement in March 2009 to the effect that they would buy up vineyards in the region to produce a Chinese version of "grand

---

7   Ibid, p. 11
8   Ibid.

cru."⁹ This is all very exciting news for China as well as the international market. Until recent years, China's wine has been considered subpar, mainly due to the Chinese emphasis on quantity over quality, but that is all about to change as Chinese wineries now focus on the quality of their grapes and wines over mass production.

France's Influence on China's Winemaking

Yes, ladies and gentlemen, the Chinese wine market is on the rise—big time. And not just in quantity as in the years before, but now in quality as well. In Bordeaux, France, the Bordeaux International Wine Institute offers training in enology (study of winemaking). When it first opened in 2004, there were only twenty students and most of them came from France. Currently, there are over one hundred students enrolled in the winemaking class.¹⁰ The interesting thing about the 2014 class is not its size, but who is attending. There are some students from countries such as Turkey and India, but 30% of the class is Chinese. This is the largest group of students by nationality in attendance after the French. By contrast, there were less than 4% Americans enrolled in the class.

Dijon's Burgundy Business School has received a higher number of Chinese students recently, too. In

---

9 Ibid, p. 13

10 http://www.nytimes.com/2014/01/26/opinion/sunday/chinas-new-obsession-french-wine.html

2015, over 30% of the students enrolled in the class were Chinese. Why has there been an increase of Chinese studying wine in France? With wine being a rich tradition in French culture and a growing middle class in China drinking wine, the Chinese are studying in France to enhance their wine-making skills.[11] However, along with this increase in Chinese students learning the timeworn tradition of the French enological arts, there is a deep-rooted fear in France that China, with its teeming population and endless territory, could one day outperform and take over the French wine industry.

Due to the general absence of information about the Chinese wine industry, most are surprised to learn that China has a tradition of producing European-style wine going back to the 19th century. Some of the Chinese students in France did their undergraduate course work in China and interned in the Chinese wine industry before studying in France. Some grew up working on family-owned vineyards, or sold wine at shops owned by their family. Most of these students, regardless of their background, go back to China after studying in France and bring a respect for French culture back to their homeland which they impart to their people.

The true advantage this influx of Chinese students gives to France is an economic one. Almost half of the wine that is imported into China is from France, and Bordeaux's red wine is a favorite among the Chinese

---

11 Ibid.

fortunate enough to be able to drink it.[12] This is similar to what happened in the 1950s and '60s when French wine-making skills were taken to California, which started a new interest in French wine and culture throughout America. French winemaking techniques combined with the fact that the Chinese wine market can only grow creates a tremendous advantage for budding French-Chinese relations. In the summer of 2013, VinExpo in Bordeaux predicted a growth in Chinese wine intake by 40% between 2012 and 2016.[13] China is one of the top five export markets for French burgundy wine. The French should see this as a good thing, and I am sure they do.

    Chinese investors have been buying Bordeaux chateaus at a rate of about one per month. It caused concern in France when a Chinese company bought Château Bellefont-Belcier, a grand cru wine producer. Of course, this should not be a real concern because there are over 8,000 properties in France that are predominantly French-owned.[14] And France, as I mentioned before, has been investing in China, too. Both the French and Chinese should be optimistic as they have a lot to gain from one another in this rapid push toward globalization. This is not going to destroy the French wine industry at all, or the Chinese industry for that matter, but it will enrich both of them with cultural links that enliven and distinguish

---

12 Ibid.
13 Ibid.
14 Ibid.

each country in ways not previously imagined by either.

Of course, not all the French see this influx of Chinese investors buying up their wineries as a bad thing. Some prefer it was them than the Parisians. One leading winemaker said, "I don't care who buys these chateaus, as long as they are not from Paris."[15]

China's Wine Market

Some of the experts say that the reason China became the world's leading consumer of red wine has more to do with culture than with taste. In China, red is considered extremely lucky and it is also the color associated with the government. China is not alone in thinking red to be the luckiest of colors. Throughout history across the globe, red has been considered very lucky. In ancient times, Alexander the Great is reported to have believed that the gods favored those who wore red, which led many a general and king to follow suit by wearing the color. Most national flags across the globe have red in them, but the dominance of red in China is even more pronounced than perhaps in any other culture in the world. It is associated with the planet Mars and the element of fire and, for the Chinese, it is also a symbol of happiness and good fortune.

Apart from the health benefits of drinking red wine in comparison to the excessive consumption of grain-based alcohol, the success of red wine in China

---

15 Ibid.

has strong cultural ties to the color red. According to the CEO of Vinexpo, Guillaume Deglise, the color red symbolizes wealth, power and luck, and these three values are fundamental in sealing partnerships in the business world. He added that in China, "White is the color of death. So you don't want to drink white, why would you?"[16]

However, people in China are slowly starting to enjoy white wine. According to Vinexpo, the consumption of white wines, including sparkling wines, will increase as the market matures in China over the next few years. An article on Bloomberg.com by Elin McCoy about the Vinexpo 2015 caught my attention and lifted my spirits. It was titled "Top Chinese Wines Have Gone from Bad to Good. Will They Become Great?"[17]

Near the beginning of her article she states:

"People outside China don't know much about these wines because so few have been exported. Only in the past couple of years have a handful grabbed medals in international wine competitions and gained media attention. Many others were (and still are) poor, thin, lacked fruit, and often suffered from basic winemaking faults."

---

[16] Rueters (January 28, 2014). *Chinese become world's top tipplers of 'lucky' red wine*. Available from http://www.reuters.com/article/us-beverages-wine-china-idUSBREA0R1QO20140128

[17] McCoy, Elin (June 26, 2015). *Top Chinese Wines Have Gone from Bad to Good. Will They Become Great?* Bloomberg.com. Available from http://www.bloomberg.com/news/articles/2015-06-26/top-chinese-wines-have-gone-from-bad-to-good-will-they-become-great-

Elin writes, "To my surprise, all 17 whites, reds, and sweeties poured were impressive. Although I didn't find a great one, I did find several very good wines well worth trying."

The article goes on to point out that the purpose of the tasting was to heighten the image of Chinese wine and persuade international wine traders that the Chinese are not simply content to "knock back bling bottles" of costly French wine. I like her phrasing because it is a language I can understand. More importantly, she is illustrating the first steps the world is taking toward mainstream acceptance of wine produced in China. This event showed the world how serious the Chinese are about going for a top spot on the world's wine map. There is also a wine building boom that is happening across Northern China where big Chinese companies have been investing heavily in colossal French-style wine chateaus in every region of the country. The international wine community is starting to take notice that China is sincere about producing quality wine.

According to Vinexpo statistics, more than 91% of wines consumed in China are red. McCoy noted that during the tasting she found several white wines that had potential. The most popular grape in China is cabernet sauvignon, but there is a new focus on aglianico and syrah. McCoy said she was most impressed by various wines from Changyu, the oldest and largest of China's commercial wineries, which had planted vineyards with imported vine cuttings from France. As we have established, the Chinese wine market is dominated by red wine, which of course we know China loves. While I love red wine too, I don't agree with how most wine analysts, writers, and consultants believe the only future for wine in China is red.

Now, don't get me wrong. Red wine is nice, it's wholesome, it's good, and in many cases it is preferable to white wine. However, I believe the future of wine in China is both red and white. I would ask that if red wine is preferred because it is the same color as the color of luck, why has it only been a favorite in the last twenty or thirty years of China's history? In contrast, baijiu, which is white in color, is China's most popular alcoholic beverage that has been consumed by its people for thousands of years. Moreover, there is strong evidence to support the fact that Chinese people may actually prefer white wine to red.

Ma Huiqun, a molecular biologist and wine marketing expert, has conducted polls in China and found that the Chinese prefer white wine to red at a ratio of two to one. Jim Boyce found that wine drinkers at blind tastings over the past five years have given white wines equal, if not better, scores than what they gave to red wines. Helene Ponty of Le Ponty in Bordeaux said her white wine samples disappear at tastings before the red wine samples do, although reds typically outsell whites at the same events.18 Further

---

18 Boyce, Jim (November 27, 2014). *China loves red wine, but white may become more popular.* Southern China Morning Post. Available from http://www.scmp.com/lifestyle/food-wine/article/1650018/china-loves-red-wine-white-may-become-more-popular.

evidence of the rise of white wine in China is the current expansion of white wine production in the Ningxia region, particularly the Silver Heights Winery, which is run by the famed wine-maker Emma Gao, who recently produced her first chardonnay.

Will white ever outsell red? I do not believe this will ever happen for a few reasons. White wine has a shorter shelf life compared to red wine. Many people hail the '82 Bordeaux as the pinnacle of what red wine should be. Why is it that we have never heard of a famous '82 white wine vintage? If we were to drink it today, it would not be good because how long a wine can be stored has a lot to do with the way it was produced. Red wine has a longer maturation potential because of tannins which are a naturally occurring polyphenol found in plants, seeds, bark, wood, leaves, and fruit skins.

What distinguishes between red and white wine? It is not just the color but the contact the wine has with the grape skins, seeds and stems. Tannins are imparted into the wine from these impurities. Some phenols are also imparted into the wine from wood barrel fermentation and oak-aging. This is why red wine can be kept for many years. This is why red wine ages well and white wine will perish after only a few short years.

The second reason white will never outsell red ties into the first in that when red wine ages, it increases in value. Investing in red wine, especially rare vintages, is a reasonable investment that will increase in value if the wine is stored properly and kept in excellent condition. You simply cannot do this with white wine. Finally, though I am reluctant to admit it, the majority of great wine in the market is red. This is because the big name producers all make more red wine than white wine.

Furthermore, Chinese businessmen are very risk-averse and cabernet sauvignon is what sells, so we can expect this wine to be the cornerstone of the market for some time to come. However, things change and, with the increased sampling of white wine and the expansion in its production and the growth of chardonnay and other grapes for white wine, more people in China will enjoy white wine, but it will not outsell red. This is not only an exciting time in the history of China's wine culture for the future of red wine. It is a very exciting time for the future of white wine, too.

Chapter 3

Current and Cultural Landscape

China's economic boom over the last decade has led to massive changes in the consumption of alcoholic drinks. The rapid economic growth has enabled more and more Chinese people to buy more than just beer and baijiu. They have become interested in what is available from foreign markets. They have also been able to go out more which has led to the opening of more pubs in China. Most importantly, rising incomes have directly correlated with the Chinese middle class embracing a wine culture, which many consider a fashionable Western drink. The newfound financial independence of many women may also account for the rise in wine drinking among them. Additionally, Chinese women are leaning towards wine as their drink of choice because it suits their ambitious lifestyles. There is also the current perception in China that wine drinking is good for one's health. I agree—and if it increases the beauty of one's skin—why not?

After a decade of uninterrupted growth, the Chinese wine market has further slowed down in 2015 during a big recession that started in 2013. Even though China is currently the fifth largest wine market in the world, its domestic wines have been declining. Experts have different views as to why local Chinese wines have had negative growth. An owner of a winery in west China attributes local wines experiencing low sales to their high prices compared to some imported wines that are priced competitively lower. Stephen Li, one of the most respected wine educators in China, believes that the well educated middle class consumers who have the buying power are now able to read wine labels on imported bottles and are leaning more towards purchasing imported wines.

According to a survey of world wine and spirits consumption by Vinexpo, imported wines have had a positive growth of 3.3% in volume between 2013 and 2014. French wines make up 42% of the market share and Australian wine holds second place in China. In addition, Champagne, which was not affected by the anti-corruption campaign, has seen its volume double between 2010 and 2014.

A study by economists at the University of Adelaide's Wine Economics Research Center provides a silver lining, which projects China's wine consumption to grow between 40% and 60% between 2011 and 2018. Professor Kym Anderson, Executive Director of the Wine Economics Research Center said that from 2011 to 2018, China's net wine imports could grow between 330 and 790 million litters with the help of the country's bilateral free trade agreement with Australia, Chile and New Zealand. In addition to what the experts are saying, I believe that some of the following underlying factors will also support the growth and maturity of China's wine market in the coming years.

E-commerce

With nearly 800 million internet participants, China's potential is vast with consumers gaining access to fair market prices for a variety of brands, wherever they may be located. Ian Ford, co-founder and general manager of Summergate, one of the leading wine providers across Greater China, has noted that his company has seen sales triple to e-commerce operators. "Previously, consumers only had access to wine in their local superstore where the options to buy well-stored wine that was well- priced was virtually nil.[19]" Popular online websites like Jiuxian.com, Jingdong (JD.com) and Tmall.com allow wine merchants to meet the demand of Chinese consumers.

Lately, the Alibaba Group has been playing a major role in the way the Chinese wine market has been growing and bringing more options to the Chinese wine enthusiast. Jack Ma founded the website Alibaba.com in 1999 as a means to connect Chinese manufacturers with overseas buyers.

---

[19] Schmitt, Patrick (January 8, 2015). *China Wine Industry Suffers 'Shakeout'*. The Drinks Business. Available from https://www.thedrinksbusiness.com/2015/01/china-wine-industry-suffers-shakeout/.

Interestingly enough, the Alibaba Group sought an initial public offering in the USA, giving American stock holders a chance to buy a share of the company. Due to the Chinese government's ban on foreign ownership, all shares were purchased in a Cayman Islands shell corporation. Alibaba.com was primed for take-off just the same and now the group hosts a myriad of portals that make all manner of international e-commerce possible. Tmall.com, an online storefront owned by the Alibaba Group, is one of several major sellers of wine to the Chinese market.

Consider the online market as an indicator of China's expanding wine market of the future. Jiuxian.com, China's largest online alcohol retailer, was officially listed on China's National Equities Exchange and Quotations. This new listing recognizes the company's success due to completing several rounds of equity financing, and its six years of rapid development has shown a great significance for its future. In addition to being the leader in the online alcohol retailing industry, the company also follows the alcohol industry's development trends, which makes it an important indicator to industry changes. Overall, this has boosted the valuation and importance of the online alcohol retailing market in China.

The integration of modern technology into the marketplace infers these markets will expand. John Watkins, CEO of ASC Fine Wines, noted he has seen wine sales make up 34% of online sales in his company, while noting only a 5% increase in the offline world of alcohol. He credits this difference with younger consumers and most notably, empowered women.[20]

Wine Education and Marketing

In Beijing, Ma Huiqin has been giving lessons in wine tasting for over 10 years. She currently tutors more than 400 students. Ma said few distributors expected expensive wine sales to rise quickly. She said, "When I started teaching, only a few people would have tasted wine. When you asked about tastes they would say sweet and sour. Now more than half have experienced wine before they come to my class."

"Young people are a very strong driving force ... Chinese people want to try something interesting and new. Pizza has been very successful; KFC has been very successful. Twenty years ago very few Chinese drank coffee, but now so many do." Ma, a microbiologist at China Agricultural University and an expert on wine marketing, said that the numbers over-estimated the true level of consumption since distributors and retailers kept a tremendous amount of unsold stock. "For most Chinese it is still an occasional commodity, mainly for holidays. There will be more consumers, but they are occasional

---

20 Chow, Jason (July 13, 2014). *China's Wine Market Shift Toward Entry Level*. The Wall Street Journal. Available from http://www.wsj.com/articles/chinas-wine-market-shifts-toward-entry-level-1405305923.

consumers," she said.[21] Jim Boyce from the famous Chinese wine blog, The Grape Wall of China said, "The average is [about] one bottle a year per person. But the scale of China makes it a huge market."[22]

Nicolas Billot-Grima, who has been a winemaker within China for over 25 years, began in the Shandong province (Huadong) and now consults for several wineries. He feels that Chinese consumers will try varieties other than red wine because they are open-minded. They will try the product as long as they are well educated about it. He mentioned that white wine is less tannic as well as fruitier and easier to become accustomed to, making it great for beginners. Also, white wines pair very nicely with Chinese food.

One of the perceived weaknesses about local Chinese wine is that everything is leaning toward Cabernet. Famous critics like Jancis Robinson regularly note this focus of the Chinese wine industry. The fact is this apparent weakness is slowly being offset by the rising number of non-Cab options, several of which come from Grace Vineyards, a winery which many think of as the country's great success story of the last decade.

Of the bunch that they produce, marselan is one of the frontrunners, which Jim Boyce thinks might

---

21 Willsher, Kim (January 29, 2014). *China becomes biggest market for red wine, with 1.86bn bottles sold in 2013.* The Guardian. Available from http://www.theguardian.com/world/2014/jan/29/china-appetite-red-wine-market-boom.

22 Ibid.

someday be bestowed with the title of "China's grape.[23]" Grace Vineyard's CEO Judy Chan spoke with Jim Boyce about the rise of marselan. "We always wanted to figure out where to plant and what to plant in China to figure out what is a truly Chinese-style wine. Of course, it's not going to happen within the next five to ten years, but somebody had to start somewhere and that's why we started planting not only marselan, but also other varietals," she said.[24]

In 2015 she spoke about Grace Vineyards launching marselan, aglianico, and syrah. Three new varietals other than Cabernet Sauvignon mark just one of the ways in which the winery is branching off, away from the traditional focus of the Chinese wine industry. Marselan, she explained is "spicier, bigger, and more concentrated."[25] With a much higher alcohol content it is quite a lot different from what they usually offer in China.

Grace Vineyards' other wines are lighter and fruitier and by contrast the marselan has a much more distinct, different taste than most of the others. Grace also has sparkling wine being produced, which was launched in August of 2015. Two types of them were released, an entry level sparkler that goes by the name

---

23 Boyce, Jim (May 19, 2015). *Beyond Cabernet: Grace Vineyard to release Marselan, Aglianico and more.* Grape Wall of China. Available from http://www.grapewallofchina.com/2015/05/19/beyond-cabernet-grace-vineyard-to-release-marselan-aglianico-and-more/.

24 Ibid.

25 Ibid.

of Angie and the reserve, Angelina. With the reserve, Judy said, they tried to concentrate more on minerality and acidity, and give less focus to the nutty taste. Angie, the entry level wine, is more approachable, according to Judy.[26]

Tradeshows and Events

Chris Roberts, general manager at the Double Tree by Hilton Guangzhou, talked about the inaugural food and wine experience in Guangzhou he organized in 2015. Having been in Guangzhou for two and a half years, most of which time was spent opening the hotel that has now been open for over a year, made him realize what a great idea it would be to put on a cultural event here. He says, "I find Guangzhou is now far more advanced than Beijing was 12 years ago when I first arrived before the Olympics. It's more advanced as a food and beverage market but given its proximity to Hong Kong, it's so far behind Beijing and Shanghai for wine. I find it's a city for beer, but not so much for wine."[27]

Roberts went on to say that what they are doing is a carbon copy of what they did in Beijing, with a concentration on the educational aspects that are

---

26 Ibid.

27 Boyce, Jim (May 15, 2015). *Chris Roberts on the inaugural Food & Wine Experience at DoubleTree by Hilton Guangzhou*. Grape Wall of China. Available from http://www.grapewallofchina.com/2015/05/15/chris-roberts-on-the-first-doubletree-by-hilton-guangzhou-food-wine-experience/.

affordable. Three hours are dedicated to trade and four to the public, which includes a buffet. Plus, there are ten tasting classes. With over 500 products from 148 suppliers, this is no small event. Hearing about the grand scale of the operation is something that should prick the ears of any wine enthusiast, no matter where he or she hails from. There are three zones: Europe, Asia-Pacific, and South Africa. Chinese wines are included in the Asia-Pacific zone. They also have products from the rest of the world too, but on a much smaller scale.

Tim Adams, the owner and winemaker at Tim Adams Wines (in Clare Valley, South Australia) did two tasting sessions: one for the trade, and one for the public and media. He included a tasting of eight wines which express his diverse range, including five reds and three whites. All of it was very casual and informal. Tim Adams always puts on a friendly show in his classy, understated manner. "He's a very down to earth guy," said Chris Roberts.

Ningxia hosted the Site Vinitech trade show for two days in June 2015. This is the second year Ningxia has hosted the event and the Mendoza region in Argentina will host it in 2016. Site Vinitech encompassed everything from bottles and barrels to vineyard equipment and nurseries. There was also a series of brief presentations by members of a French delegation. Among the topics included were barrel aging, vineyard management, and wine filtration. There was a big selection of wine labels on display for the crowds of oenophiles that came to taste the variety of wines.

Radoux, a barrel supplier, and Diam, a closure maker, worked together to host a barbeque for winemakers. The barbeque was hosted at the Kempinski Hotel in Ningxia the day before the trade show began. XiXia King, Leirenshou, Chandon, and Legacy Peak were among those wine producers who brought wine to the event to taste. The barbeque provided for an interesting microcosm of the modern day wine industry in China.

The subtle differences, as well as the big ones, underscore just how far the quality of wine has come from the Chinese industry. There is an increasing diversity in the Chinese wine scene that is interesting to watch. According to Jim Boyce, some of the best wine at the trade show included Helan Qing Xue and Lan Ding's Cabernet.[28]

In September 2015, the two-year Ningxia Winemakers Challenge (NWC) involved about sixty participants with a prize pool of RMB 840,000 ($135,000 USD). This is over a fourfold increase in prize money that was offered in the inaugural project from 2012-2014. People from over twelve countries applied for the 2015 challenge the first week it was opened for enrollment.

---

28 Boyce, Jim (June 10, 2015). *BBQ party: Radoux, Diam host winemakers event in Ningxia*. Grape Wall of China. Available from http://www.grapewallofchina.com/2015/06/10/bbq-party-radoux-diam-host-winemakers-event-in-ningxia/.

The NWC is organized and operated by the International Federation of Vine and Wine of Helan Mountain's East Foothill, in association with the Ningxia Grape Industry Development Bureau. About sixty successful applicants convened in Ningxia on September 20th for the launch of the project and stayed for two weeks to pick their grapes and commence on producing their wine. The wines that are produced will be judged in 2017. The first NWC had participants from seven countries.

Wine Distributors

The wine distribution channel is playing a key role in not only importing wine into China but also educating the Chinese consumer about wine. ASC Fine Wines is the largest premium wine importer and distributor in China. Not only does it focus on importing wine into China, it also runs its own wine school and further builds its credibility in China by certifying wine professionals.

A major marketing change is that New World wines are showcased in Hong Kong in a grand and spectacular fashion. Old World wine used to dominate the market in China, but now New World wine finds itself in an even mix with that of the old world. This is a major change in the industry. It used to be the case that most people thought it was fun to try New World wine, a kind of enlivening distraction, but that was at a time when the market was mostly Old World.

Today, the nature of the game has changed. New World wine is big on the market and is here to stay. It has become fifty-fifty between Old World and New World, and people are noticing that the quality of the New World wine is soaring to new heights and is now equal to the quality in the rest of the world. He recalls that sommeliers did not really exist back in 2000 and had very basic wine knowledge. Today, he sees sommeliers on a regular basis and a majority of them study at the Wine & Spirits Education Trust (WSET).

Summergate Fine Wines built a reputation as one of the leading wine providers across greater China. Founded by Ian Ford and Brendan O'Toole, the company works directly with several thousand retail buyers and hundreds of downstream distributors. They only work with brands that have the best reputation, quality, and value for money.

In an interview with the Beverage Trade Network, Ian Ford gave some great insight for people looking to enter the wine market in China. Ian said it is very important to find a strong, experienced and honest importer to partner with. The importer should be able to provide genuine market intelligence on the whole country, build and defend the brand, build relevant and sustainable distribution that is transparent, manage an honest pricing structure, and keep an open dialogue about opportunities, threats and strategies. He warned to be careful of the majority of importer-distributors in China that are seeking short-term and opportunistic profits.[29]

Bars and Restaurants

Of course, the infrastructure for large-scale production and luxury consumption is in place for China's apparent world domination, but there can be no better indication of what's really going on than taking a look at the smaller players on the burgeoning wine scene, namely wine bars. Despite the government austerity and social stigmas associated with wealth, wine bars are booming. Take Dr. Wine, Shanghai's "favorite wine bar," featuring two stories of conviviality, catering to sharply dressed twenty- and thirty-somethings. Not to be outdone, there's Roosevelt's Wine Cellar, boasting not only the largest wine cellar in Shanghai, but in the world. In Beijing, there's Bordeauxthéque, boasting one of the most specialized collections of Bordeaux-based wines in the city, if not the entire country. Smaller wine bars without large-scale ambitions certainly proliferate throughout the city, creating the impression there's simply no difference between China and the rest of the world.

High-end hotels and restaurants in Shanghai stock some of China's premier wines, sourced both from

---

[29] *China Uncovered: Interview With One Of The Largest Wine Importers In China.* Beverage Trade Network. Available from http://beveragetradenetwork.com/en/btn-academy/articles/china-uncovered-interview-with-one-of-the-largest-wine-importers-in-china-330.htm.

Yantai and Xinjiang. Wines produced in Ningxia have been awarded accolades on an international level from Decanter Magazine. A number of other wines have also received positive reviews from Robert Parker, a prominent US wine critic who scored 18 of 20 Chinese wines on his own scale as average or better.

"I think as consumers increasingly buy based on taste, we are going to see more diversity in terms of grape varieties, and we'll hopefully see which do best in China," says Jim Boyce[30], founder of the wine blog, Grape Wall of China.

Guidelines for Exporting Wine to China

More and more consumers are becoming affluent as the Chinese economy continues to experience rapid growth. More people are drinking wine, especially the younger middle class millennials. Middle-aged people who are health conscious are also drinking more red wine. The increasing desire for quality wine shows the expanding tastes among the new generation of Chinese drinkers and is a major force behind the growth of wine imports to fill this growing demand.

With the ever increasing growth in the Chinese wine market, more and more foreign wine producers have embarked upon the industry, targeting the up-market wine drinking culture. In 2015, foreign

---

30 Ibid.

winemakers made up about 15% of the total number of enterprises.[31]

Now let's take a closer look at what drives growth.

With the newfound rapid growth of the wine industry in China and revenue expanding at an annual rate of 4.3% in the last five years, wine drinkers' tastes are moving in the direction of drinks with a lesser alcohol content. For that reason, as well as for health benefits, wine is being consumed by an ever expanding group of people. This, along with the fact that the average per capita income is rapidly increasing, is the reason we are seeing such a huge growth in the Chinese wine industry. Outside investors are seeing the large growth potential in both industry development and domestic demand.

With Chinese people of mid to high level incomes multiplying at such a rapid rate, the increase in China's wine demand will be maintained for the foreseeable future. In the past five years, the number of people in these groups of income levels has gone up by about 20%. Rising income levels among the younger segment of the population has equated to more people pursuing trendy Western-influenced lifestyles.

The image created by the brand creates demand among consumers who have established preferences toward wine. It used to be that wine drinkers in China preferred buying domestic wine rather than imports as large chunks of capital have been invested in brand promotion. Changyu, Dynasty, and Great Wall

---

31 Ibid.

are just a few of the most well-established brands. The situation is changing fast due to the increase in imported wine.

Foreign brands are now also aggressively promoted in China. Foreign wine producers have entered the Chinese industry to target the upscale consumer markets. Enterprises from Australia, France, Germany, Italy, New Zealand, and the United States continue to increase the amount of wine they import. These imports are predicted to grow at an annual rate of 3.2% to $1.8 billion (USD) by 2020. This will account for nearly 20% of China's domestic demand.

The amount of imported wine in the domestic market has increased in recent years, its value reaching nearly 17.4% of domestic demand in 2015. By contrast, in 2010 it was 13.8%. With import taxation decreasing and consumption taxes reduced, imported wines cost less now. This, of course, also opens up the market to foreign producers.

Still, imported products generally are more expensive than domestic ones, despite the lowering of import taxes and adjustments to tax consumption policies. The difficulties of marketing imported brands are manifold. Since 2010, foreign producer investments into market channel building and advertising was low. They chose to sell wines through agents instead of paying large fees to terminal channels. Many agents in China sell many different brands of wine and don't invest in brand development.

In 2014, sales of imported wine were very slow, slower than in previous years. Expansion of imports from Australia and Chile were good, but performance of French wine was low and its previously firm grip on the lead among foreign producers was greatly reduced. Chilean wine sales benefited from tax-free concession, which was highly beneficial to their sales. Australian wine became the new highlight of the market, mainly because its product classification is easier to understand. In contrast, French wine was cluttered in product classification. Its market performance was severely hurt by the anti-extravagance campaign due to its premium position.

The leading distributors of foreign premium wine in China are the foreign companies with the most experience of doing business in China. These companies are often approached by wine suppliers from other countries, including New Zealand, but generally don't take on additional labels unless they are backed by strong marketing and finance. Foreign exporters wishing to enter the market must make sure they have enough capital and marketing capacity before they come to these distributors.

Due to the high cost of effective large-scale marketing in China, foreign companies may focus their marketing on a specific region or city, or even target a specific demographic. A significant understanding of Chinese culture is the most important thing to have before entering the market. Also, foreign companies must keep in mind that there may be significant cultural differences among the various regions. Basically, if you don't account for these factors, don't enter the market.

This cannot be stressed enough! You must have a deep and thorough understanding of China's culture, people and the various cultures within the country. One way to introduce products to the market is through attendance at trade fairs, wine dinners, and social media campaigns (on such popular Chinese social networks as Wechat and Weibo). You can invite people to visit your country on educational wine tours while offering them the opportunity to work with boutique journalists to garner the proper exposure.

High on your list of things to do is find a distributor in China whom you can trust and who is looking for a long-term partnership. If you are looking for long-term development in China, it is important to find a wine-educated partner with a strong marketing and branding capability. Your distributor needs to have marketing staff and sales people who are professional to the utmost, capable of delivering the most significant, important information about your brand. They must have very strong knowledge of wine and the ability to articulate the unique selling points of your wine.

China is a massive country and, therefore, regional distribution is a strong option for consideration. Wineries must still look for all the essentials listed above for each of the individual, regional distributors. But keep in mind, it is impossible to avoid cross-region sales of your wine. If you have a multi-distribution system across China, it is a near necessity to have a China manager who has got his or her boots on the ground and is able to handle the various distributors, managing the marketing for the different regions.

With the vastness and grandeur of China, I would like to stress considering regional distribution as your best option. Of course, this depends on what exactly your distribution goals are, but more often than not, this is the sound choice. With regards to choosing a regional distribution, wineries can reference the criteria that I listed.

As a warning, working with e-commerce platforms directly has never been favored as they are normally focused on online sales and unable to conceive, let alone develop, other sales channels such as restaurants and hotels. Bigger e-commerce companies, however, are establishing offline sales channels and are often willing to import directly from your country. Many wineries across the world should consider these opportunities.

Realistically, breaking into the Chinese market as a new wine brand is very challenging but can be very rewarding if you have done your research and partner with the right distributor. Typical wine stores in China carry major low cost California labels such as Gallo and Carlo Rossi as well as some Chinese labels such as Great Wall and Dynasty. Bars typically gravitate towards French marquee brands (Lafite, Latour, Margaux.)

In order to effectively operate in China, you will first and foremost need someone who has a thorough understanding of the culture for the region in which you are looking to sell. Unlike in more developed economies, China is simply not structured to allow unfettered international presence without boots on the ground. Language barriers, corruption, and just "not knowing who to call" will be a sampling of the issues you will run up against.

Luckily, Mandarin is one of the world's most popular languages and China's renowned University system is pumping out new, talented graduates every year. Leverage the purchasing power of the dollar by hiring a temporary business development executive directly from China, via sites such as Guru and UpWork, both of which have a number of bilingual executives from the PRC.

Firstly, hire a bilingual research assistant to create a database of potential targets. Include their contact info in a spreadsheet. Don't use Google spreadsheets or any Google products as they are banned in China.

Secondly, have all of your marketing collateral professionally translated into Mandarin. Note that the person who will handle your sales is probably not the best person to translate the marketing collateral. Writers and sales people are definitely two very different people with two very different skill-sets.

Thirdly, have a sales executive reach out to the contacts via phone. Make sure they use CRM software such as close.io, which will allow you to record their calls in real time via VOIP. Now, you won't be able to understand what they are saying, but at least you have the recordings and you can always have a Mandarin speaking friend or another contractor listen in to some random calls to make sure they are legitimate.

The Chinese executive should a have good working knowledge of the on-the-ground business culture and you should anticipate pretty significant "meals and entertainment" expenses. These potential leads will not bear fruit until months of numerous dinners and outings. That's the cost of doing business in China. Don't be surprised by the need to provide truly lavish dinners and nights out to your potential Chinese partners. The bar, in terms of what is needed to truly "court" a potential prospect, is far higher in China than in developed countries, much to the chagrin and surprise of Westerners. A typical business dinner can run as high as $500 and a typical night out, as much as $750. Consider this part of your marketing expense since traditional marketing in China is often not as effective.

Once you have a few solid pokers in the fire, plan a trip to China. Inexpensive tickets and hotels are available online. Make sure your fixer is on the ground to pick you up at the airport and work with you while you are in China. China is not for the faint of heart. Even getting out of the airport without some Mandarin is not easy. Do not expect local bus drivers or taxi drivers to speak English. That being said, it is safe, so there is no need to worry about personal safety.

Culture Tip: Seniority is very important in China. A quick survey of any group of Chinese business people will immediately reveal a hierarchy. One individual, typically an older male, will be treated with greater deference by the others. Make sure you greet him first and try to impress him rather than treating every member of the group equally, as is the custom in the US. Giving undue attention to lower level staff may cause unease and embarrassment for them as they try to divert your attentions back to the boss in order to stay in harmony with their cultural norms.

Once you are in the negotiation phase with the Chinese, expect a long and drawn out process. Do not be discouraged when their initial offer is incredulously low. China is a bargaining country and as in any negotiation, a good negotiator will set a very low floor, putting you at an immediate disadvantage. Make sure you have some sort of framework established before arriving in-country. In the span of a short business trip, you are at a disadvantage because the Chinese can simply stall towards the end of your trip, resulting in pressure to reach some sort of agreement.

Culture Tip: The exchange of business cards in China is quite a bit more formalized than in the U.S. Having a very nice business card will impress your Chinese colleagues. Also, when receiving a card, make sure to take it with both hands and make eye contact with the giver. Thank them for the card and put it into a business card holder, not your pocket.

Once you get them to agree to a price and even a contract, keep in mind that it is not iron-clad. Unlike in the West, contracts are considered fluid in China and subject to change later based on circumstances. The key is to remain playful, kind, and open-minded with your Chinese colleagues even when they do things that are seemingly "shady" or "two-faced" by American standards. The intention is not to be deceptive, but to realize the best deal. This wheeling and dealing is part of Chinese business culture and is not considered backhanded in any way. In fact, it is often done respectfully and even playfully.

Once the agreement is set in place and you have begun distribution, you will have to deal with tariffs. You will also come up against fake wine or people rebottling your wine, which can happen even to a small boutique brand such as France's Rafi.

As the deal continues, make sure to frequently check in with your Chinese colleagues, because communication is key. Since there is a time zone difference, expect to chat in the early morning or early evening. Consider downloading the WeChat application on your phone since everyone in China uses that and it's a great way to stay in touch. Use chat and IM communication, not VOIP or phone calls, as your Chinese colleagues will likely be far more comfortable communicating via IM versus voice.

"With patience comes success,"[32] said Jeff Harder, the managing director of Ex Nihilo Vineyards. He's quoting a famous Chinese proverb, one of definite significance to North American wineries seeking to penetrate the Asian market. Ex Nihilo, one of several Canadian wineries present at the Hong Kong International Wine and Spirits fair, has a Hong Kong distributor.

Jeff put special emphasis on the fact that establishing a strong trading relationship in China doesn't happen

---

32 Lavin, Kate (January 2012). *The Slow Boat to China: Entertaining the Asian wine market takes time.* Wines and Vines. Available from http://www.winesandvines.com/template.cfm?section=features&content=95708.

overnight. Finding an ideal business partner takes a large investment of money and, perhaps even more importantly, time. Jeff added, "[You're not] going to run over there tomorrow and find somebody to distribute your wines." It's not like the North American mentality of jumping on a great investment immediately. Asian businesspeople are more likely to take a step back and think over the deal (not to mention the very necessary negotiating stage, in which your price will always be too high).

Jeff's 4,100-case premium wine brand also has Japanese distribution. "Once you agree on a price, your business partner can be for life. When they make a commitment and give you a number in terms of wine and case sales, they will follow through on that," Jeff said of mainland China distributors. "Hong Kong is a little different. It's faster than mainland China, but they're still cautious before making any large commitments."[33]

The USDA says this about exporting wine to China:

1. The domestic company designates an agency (usually an import and export company;)
2. The import and export company signs an export contract with right of wine monopoly and an overseas wine trader;
3. An export license is secured from the Ministry of Foreign Trade and Economic Cooperation

---

33 Ibid.

when an import license for the particular wine (brandy, whisky, liqueur) is required;

4. Complete a Certificate of Origin;
5. Hygiene Certificate is issued by port supervisory and monitoring body on food hygiene and quality;
6. Customs' supervision, imposition of tariffs and other duties dealt with as well as inspection to prevent and counter smuggling in accordance with relevant laws.

Consumer demand in China is obviously growing at breakneck speeds, so those wineries that are willing and able to invest the money and time needed to go into the Asian market have certainly chosen the right time to do so. David Andrews of ASC Fine Wines Trading Corp. (general manager for Hong Kong and Macau), has revealed that wines currently hold a market share of 25% in China[34]. The flip side of this news is that North American wineries have reaped little benefit from this high level of demand.

However, as we have noted, more and more North American wineries are setting up deals for distribution in mainland China. They are learning the ways of the Chinese market and are negotiating deals that are good for the partners on both sides of the Pacific while expanding their knowledge base of how the Chinese wine market works and finding the best ways to work within the confines of the market to expand awareness

---

34 Ibid.

of their particular brands. At times, this has been a painstakingly slow and arduous process, but in the end it will inevitably prove well worth the effort as the market in China is vast and ever expanding and the people are curious and remain open to trying new wine.

Credit: Discover Hong Kong Tourism

Due to the vastness of China and the grand scale of its wine market, few North American wineries can hope to have a significant presence across the country. For most of them, what they need to do is find the right niche.

As far as the bigger wine companies are concerned, a handful of prominent wine corporations are chasing prospects to the other end of the Pacific as well. Jackson Family Wines is present in over 70 global markets.[35] These statistics come from Nick Bevan, senior vice president of international distribution and sales. The company's priority Asian markets include China, Japan, Hong Kong, South Korea, and Singapore. "We definitely think there is a huge opportunity in

---

35 Ibid.

the Chinese market, and demand for wine is growing exponentially," said Julia Jackson, a Jackson family representative. "Hong Kong in particular is a very sophisticated wine market, where we want to showcase the highest end wines we have in our portfolio."[36]

The long, arduous task of doing business in Asia is a double-edged sword for large companies that receive sizeable orders. Jackson stated that marketing trips abroad generate a good number of leads for the company's wine. However, the corporate arm behind its 35-plus wineries researches importers from overseas before forming any definite agreements.

Globally, larger corporations have greater access to Asia's wine-drinking public. Large deals on supplies and materials cut down the average bottle cost, which is of great importance in China. While income levels vary tremendously, the per capita average is less than $8,500 per year. Moreover, unlike the chateaus of France that are selling bottles for high prices at pricey restaurants in Shanghai and Hong Kong, Canadian and U.S. wineries often find themselves grouped together with other New World wine producers.

"Distributors go into other world markets and buy Argentine and Chilean wines for amazing prices, as we know those countries can offer," said Jeff Harder, managing director of Ex Nihilo Vineyards[37]. This is a patience game.

---

36 Ibid.

37 Ibid.

CHAPTER 4

FAKE WINE

The Chinese wine boom has not been without its negatives; namely fake wines. Along with Russia, China can lay claim to having one of the largest black markets for fake and counterfeit alcohol. John Watkins, while discussing ASC Fine Wines' involvement in ensuring customer guarantees and trust, has cited how his company followed in the footsteps of other counterfeited industries – cigarette companies and the NBA (National Basketball Association) — affixing a QR code and a hologram on each of their bottles. This measure allows smartphone-equipped consumers to know exactly when the bottle left the winery and hit store shelves.

Norwegian company Thinfilm goes one step further, counteracting counterfeiters by indicating when a bottle was opened using a smartphone app, to determine if that bottle of Cabernet wasn't a Sauvignon Blanc in its past life. These measures ensure that consumers aren't duped by inferior brands and allow wine to enjoy its inherent luxury status. This problem of fake wine has increasingly plagued the wine market in China, but in recent years the government has cracked down and taken increasingly strong measures to tackle the problem and eradicate it. Let's have a look.

Suzanne Mustacich of the Wine Spectator reported on October 8, 2015:

China's thriving counterfeit wine sales have pushed advisors at the French Foreign Trade Advisory Board to quietly leak a controversial report on fake wines in the Asian nation, despite opposition by French government officials. The report details the depth of the counterfeit problem, showing that fake wines are not just the work of a few criminal rings but a sizable underground industry.[38]

The Comité National des Conseillers du Commerce Extérieur de la France (CNCCEF) is a public group of foreign trade advisors from a variety of industries which are all appointed by the foreign minister of France. The group's website says: "For more than 115 years, on a voluntary basis, they have been placing their experience at the service of France's economic presence around the world." A subgroup of theirs is the Wine & Spirits Commission.

China is, of course, not the world's only source of counterfeit wine, but the country's phenomenal growth

---

38 Mustacich, Suzanne (October 8, 2015). *How Big Is China's Counterfeit-Wine Problem? French Report Calls It An Industry.* Wine Spectator. Available from http://www.winespectator.com/webfeature/show/id/52194.

in the wine industry and weak intellectual property laws have made it the perfect breeding grounds for a huge market in fake vino. CNCCEF's investigation was born of the fact that France is one of the main exporters of wine to China. Wine Spectator's sources report that group's findings were suppressed for two years by French political leaders, after a storm exploded when the Wine & Spirits Commission revealed the estimated volume of counterfeit French wine sweeping onto the market in China. Edouard Marienbach, Track and Trace tech expert and an author of the report said, "Counterfeiting is a touchy subject. Everyone knows more or less what is at stake, but for the brands it can be a very difficult subject to deal with."[39]

The advisors recently released a report which includes ambitious proposals for using technology, legal action, job training, and communications as countermeasures. The commission reported, "The CNCCEF believes it's their job to publish this study despite the opposition from an important wine council and the Minister of Agriculture."

Their eye-popping assessment of the situation is incredible. "For every real bottle of French wine in China, there is at least one counterfeit bottle of French wine, and the situation is only getting worse. It's enormous," James de Roany, the former president of the CNCCEF Wine & Spirits commission, said. "The situation of imported French wine and spirits in China has deteriorated significantly since 2014." The problem

---

39 Ibid.

has obviously contributed to a huge drop in sales. The report blamed this drop on predatory pricing, high taxes, and discovery of other wine regions. More than anything else, it blamed Chinese consumers' mistrust of wine believed to be "too often...counterfeit."

"We therefore feel [it is] all the more important to spread this study so that precise and operational measures can be quickly implemented to stem the scourge of counterfeiting."[40]

Abandoned chicken farms have been converted to illegal bottling lines. Stories like this often headline newspapers. However, the report makes the case for a more insidious business environment. It alleges that in China, the primary counterfeiters are distributors, sub-distributors, and importers with the goal of cutting down on their purchase price, increasing volume of a particular "brand" or "brands," and altogether skipping out on import taxes and duties which can cause a rise in cost of as much as 48%. "This is where you see the industrialization of counterfeiting," de Roany said. "It's generally a very high quality, which makes it very difficult to tell the real from the fake."

Another insidious practice, perhaps equally damaging, is "brand squatting," or obtaining the Chinese rights to a foreign wine's name—this is also on the up and up, according to the commission's report. No region, brand, or grape is safe from this illicit practice. "All of the Greek grape variety names were recently the object of a trademark request, which costs little for

---

40 Ibid.

private individuals," the report said. Cognac, Scotch, and wine from all countries are vulnerable. Chinese spirits and wines face the same battle. "It is widely acknowledged that some domestic wines are diluted to four times their volume."

The state-owned food conglomerate COFCO won a case in the Wujiang District People's Court in Suzhou against 27 local supermarkets because they were selling counterfeit bottles of COFCO's Great Wall wine. Many of the defendants settled, but some claimed they had been given proper paperwork from the companies selling the fake wine.

Chinese authorities are starting to hear the voices of foreign brand owners.

According to Suzanne Mustacich of the Wine Spectator, in August, the owner of a wine company in Yantai, his wife and six partners were convicted of making and selling wine with counterfeit labels of well-known foreign wines. Their operation had started out as a legitimate company, importing bulk wine and bottling it under their own brands, but they soon realized they could make more money selling counterfeits of well-known brands. The accused received prison terms ranging from two years to four and a half years in prison and fines of up to $161,000.[41]

"For me, the most important element is our proposal to penalize the distributor for receiving and dealing in stolen goods," explained de Roany. "In China, they are likely to hand down severe sentences to

---

41 Ibid.

make an example. Thus, there is an issue of political will and that is why my colleagues at the CNCCEF believe we should publish the study. Raising awareness of the reality of the damage of counterfeiting is for them—and for me—the best way to get things done."[42]

De Roany was let go from his longstanding appointment at the CNCCEF approximately two months after giving his account and estimate of the volume of counterfeits available at a London wine trade conference. What he said angered several Bordeaux winery owners and the region's trade group. And rightly so, but perhaps he should have been taken more seriously. "We have to stop giving numbers to counterfeits. Anyone who does is a liar," explained Fabian Bova, director of the CIVB, arguing that the illegal trade is impossible to quantify precisely. The commission admits that stats on illicit trade are not available but evaluations within a specific range can be given, much as they are for the drug trade.

The report and subsequent decision to publish it received unanimous support during the CNCCEF plenary meeting held at the Château Smith-Haut-Lafitte during Vinexpo 2013. The report's release has the full support of the French Foreign Trade Minister and the CNCCEF, but not that of the French government, at least not openly.

"I am astonished that the CIVB and the minister of agriculture have done everything in order to block this study without even talking with the authors," Gerard

---

42 Ibid.

Deleens said, honorary president of the China section of the CNCCEF. "I have the impression that they've fired on the ambulance."[43]

Police Destroy Fake Wine in China

In 2013, Yanti police, along with the help of Western anti-counterfeiting agents, raided a massive wine counterfeiting operation that held over $32M USD worth of wine (7,000 cases). The most popular counterfeit was Lafite Rothschild. The operation was on an industrial scale with confiscations of glass bottle molds, huge rolls of fake labels, photographs from most known major wine labels (mostly French,) corks, and all of the other essentials of a bottling plant.

China's fake alcohol problem is widely documented, with fake wine in particular being an industry on a massive scale. There are accounts of forgers openly visiting expos and tastings in order to copy label information and photograph bottle styles and colors without any resistance from the staff. Often, the perpetrators utilize attractive young female models to distract the organizers while a male accomplice snaps the pictures, sometimes discreetly and sometimes openly.

Wine writer Maureen Downey went as far as selecting her favorites from the counterfeit wines she has come across. According to Maureen, "all fakes are

---

43 Ibid.

not created equal."[44] The fake wine market has had some pretty big mistakes in producing their counterfeit products. One wonderful example is the 2008 Acker, Merrall & Condit wine auction where counterfeiter Rudy Kurniawan (currently serving time in prison) sold Domaine Ponsot wine that Laurent Ponsot later said he had never made.

This was not Rudy's only mistake. Not too long ago, he was flaunting a large bottle of old Domaine Roumier at the annual Burgundy bacchanalia in New York, La Paulée. Christophe Roumier, scion of the estate, laughed about it and said: "That is a beautiful bottle. My grandfather never made that wine, but it is a beautiful bottle."

If only Rudy had had better information, or had done some research, he would still be operating to this day. But, fortunately for the boutique wine world, he was not clever enough, and now it's time for everyone involved in the rarefied world of wine to start picking up the pieces. Rudy is, of course, not the only maker of fakes.

Over many years, Maureen has developed an eye for fake wine. Maureen says the question she is asked the most is, "What is the worst fake you have ever seen?"[45] It's a hard question for her to answer. Every time she thinks she has come across the worst, there is worse still. The issue of wine fraud is a serious one and

---

44 Downey, Maureen (June 20, 2013). *Top 12 Wine Fakes*. Wine-searcher. Available from http://www.wine-searcher.com/m/2013/06/top-12-wine-fakes.

45 Ibid.

she reports that she loves to share her best finds. She has put together a fascinating and eclectic mix of some elaborate and not so elaborate fakes.

No. 1 on her list is an 1870 Chateau Latour 6L. She found the bottle particularly interesting for many reasons. She described the size of the large bottle and its equally large label as "hilarious." Maureen says that if there were large format bottles made in 1870, producers did not make large labels to match what would have been just a few bottles. In this case, the counterfeiter went the extra length, slapping on melted crayon to mask the blank cork.

Deceptive wine vendors and fake wine apologists like to point out the various ways that silly bottles such as this could be legitimate. "The chateau could have produced it at a later date for a collector who brought in many small bottles." If that was true, the bottle would come with paperwork and a chateau-branded cork. Plus the label would be legit.

No. 2 on her list is a 1900 Barton & Guestier Chateau Lafite and Chateau Margaux. Maureen heard from U.S. billionaire Bill Koch's private investigators about the bottles of Chateau Lafite and Chateau Margaux— fake 1900 B&G wine—that started appearing for the millennium parties around the end of 1999. Too bad they have nothing to do with the chateaux, or Barton & Guestier. Instead, they were produced by a convicted forger— Khaled Rouabah, a North African native who lived in Brussels.

In 2002, it was discovered that fraudulent 1900 Margaux and Lafite wine had been auctioned off in

Paris before and after the millennium. B&G (at the time part of Seagram), Chateau Margaux, and the police of France started investigating. It turned out that good old Khaled had made these awful fakes and was convicted of fraud in a French court two years later. He appealed, as is his right, and Chateau Lafite Rothschild joined the others in pursuing legal action against him. The appeal lost and he was sentenced to a year in jail and the equivalent of a $67,000 fine. A class-action settlement at the time was obtained for all the victims. The tragic part is that the bottles Maureen encountered were both bought after Khaled was convicted.

No. 3 on the list of frauds Maureen has encountered is the 1900 Chateau Margaux 3L. A three-liter bottle she calls remarkable and not in a good way. The size alone is highly dubious and the paper does not suit the time or the winery it was claimed to be made in. The printing is also not right. Upon a closer inspection, one can see the printing is constructed of tiny dots, like those produced by a screen press, not the product of an ink press via chateau production. The "Nicolas Stamp," symbol of a famous retailer of France that aged manifold great wine, is screen-printed rather than done with an ink press. If it was an authentic label, it would be stamped on over the ink printed label after production had taken place.

Strangely, there were odd machine scuff marks all along the glass. This held true for yet another bottle of the same collection. The two bottles were obtained from the same vendor. It is likely that they came from the same infamous European wine forger. The cork in the bottle was 2 cm long, with the standard for such a bottle being 5.2 cm. The discrepancies are abundant.

No. 4 on Maureen's list of fakes was a 1928 Chateau Margaux 4.5L. It was a horrible attempt. A mark above the upper right corner of the label made it clear that there was another label on the bottle before it metamorphosed into a "1928 Chateau Margaux."

No. 5 represents a common fake Maureen comes across. It is a 1945 Chateau Mouton "RC." She claims to have likely come across more fake 1945 Moutons than were produced in the vintage. She calls many of the fakes "howlers." She's seen hundreds of magnums and 750-ml bottles of the legendary wine and she's seen 3-liter and 6-liter versions as well.

Nearly all of the fakes are "Reserve du Chateau" with a blue R.C. marker instead of a serial number. Bizarrely, she has found many differences among the examples she's come across, suggesting a multitude of counterfeiters of this variety. Found among Rudy's personal effects was an encrypted recipe for 1945 Chateau Mouton. Most of the fakes lack the necessary detail on the emblem, plus the metallic quality of the ink and the paper is wrong. Many of the fakes were lackadaisically photocopied.

Maureen's No. 6 is the 1921 Petrus 6L, which is among her favorite bottles. She came across a 6-liter 1921 Petrus a few weeks after she and Bill Koch snapped a picture following a court victory of his regarding fake wine. Eric Greenberg was found liable of fraud, ordered to pay full restitution to Koch, including damages and $12 million in punitive damages for selling fake wine while knowing he was doing so. A pivotal wine in the case was the 1921 Petrus magnum.

Authentication expert and resident of Bordeau, Michael Egan, established that, in 1921, 27 different people owned Petrus and the estate was not in good economic shape. Petrus was only really discovered in 1947 after the attention he garnered with the release of his 1945 vintage. Before that, most Petrus wine was picked up by Northern European negociants and bottled without much hoopla.

Michael testified that staff at the estate indicated they really doubt large formats were made in the time period. And, if they were, the estate did not have the money to produce large labels for what would have been a limited supply. Maureen found, under magnification, that the fake age and dark marks that show on the label were printed. It was the same sort of printing that was used for the "Nicolas Stamp." The counterfeiter was indeed lazy but Maureen surmises, probably made a good deal of money from the fakes.

Maureen's No. 7 is a 1950 Petrus "case" from an original wooden case (OWC). As she reports, she had problems with the case from the beginning. The case was sold to a collector by a company in New York City. That's bad enough, but the retailer made it worse. He gave an elaborately conceived crazy story along with the wine. Maureen had been looking at the wine bottles for around an hour when the wine buyer stopped by the inspection table. Asked about her discoveries, she brought to light a number of problems; the ink's color, the sort of paper used, and its condition, among others.

There was a problem with the capsules, she explained. "It is near impossible for 12 bottles of wine that are more than 60 years old to all have fills well into the neck and be completely lacking any real conditions of age on the labels or capsules." The collector said the bottles were sold as being chateau bottled, the merchant saying the bottles had been in their OWC up to two years before their purchase by Maureen's client. From when they were bottled (1952) to 2010, they were supposedly in the original box. The seller said that the "OWC had become so rotted that it had to be thrown out," and the bottles were then transferred to Styrofoam.

Among the 12 bottles in the case were eight examples of different bottle production. Yes, Maureen is a veritable Agatha Christie of counterfeit wine sleuthing. The glass was of different colors, shapes, sizes, methods and eras of production. Moreover, the bottles were highly irregular, hence none of them fit into any OWC. She was at a storage facility and there were plenty OWCs with which to test the bottles. If the bottles had been in an OWC, there would have been signs of decay and aging, none of which existed. There was no bin soiling or oxidation on either the glass or the labels which were all pristine apart from the fake aging that was added after the fact. The fills were perfect too.

Her client got his money back after the vender insisted on reclaiming the bottles for himself. Unfortunately, Maureen reports, the same bottles were back on the market again soon after.

My point is that these are some of the key indicators to look for when trying to determine whether a bottle is a fake or the genuine article, and Maureen gives several good examples of how she works to discover the integrity of a bottle of wine.

I'll give a couple more examples to show just how intricate forgeries can be.

No. 8 on Maureen's list is the 1961 Petrus Magnums and 6L. Many will state that Petrus is the most commonly counterfeited wine brand. It may now be different in China with Chateau Lafite claiming the top spot in recent years, but in North America and Europe, it still holds the title as far as Maureen can tell. Petrus, being faked in numerous sizes and vintages, has yielded some highly funny results (although Petrus certainly doesn't find them funny).

Maureen finds the lack of correct details in the printing quite amusing. The wrong paper, the black ink, and details of that ilk are easy tells in such blatant quackery. Something even funnier is the fact that a lot of the details in the artwork are often reversed in the printing, or mirrored. She has found many of them to be inverse images of the original art. Each time a new printing is run, more of the details are wiped out. She claims to be able to track most of the examples of fake 1961 Petrus Magnums to two specific retailers.

Maureen's No. 9 is the 1947 Chateau Lafleur 4.5L. Widely forged, the Chateau Lafleur had minimal production in the era; 17,000-18,000 bottles, or 1,400-1,500 cases a year. She finds it remarkable how many

1945, 1947, and 1950 bottles have flowed into the market in the last ten years.

One retailer of these wines emailed thousands of subscribers to tell them it was okay to have blank corks with these wines. Maureen writes that it is definitely not okay to have blank corks. Nor is it okay to have fake age and wear signs printed on them in what is obviously visible ink.

At No. 10 is the 1929 Domaine de la Romanee Conti. Maureen writes, "When you look at this label from afar, it looks a little dirty. But under magnification, it is clear to see that that "age" has been printed on. If you look at the upper right quadrant, you can see what is supposedly dirt smeared over the word "Conti." Under magnification, it becomes apparent that it is not dirt at all, but part of the printing of the label." She also states that bottle size is an issue. The bottle is not right for the time it was allegedly produced, nor was the glass age-appropriate. In this particular case, the label is all anyone needs to know that it is a fake.

At No. 11, we find the 1945 DRC Romanee Conti. The 1945 Burgundy vintage was released on a very small scale. Production was only two barrels, which turns into 600 bottles, or 50 cases. Even so, the large format 1945 bottles turn up in endless supply. Strangely enough, their look is all so similar. They have been stored together, roughed up together, with the elements of fake age all added together. Maureen humorously adds, "A particular group of drinkers known to have consumed massive quantities of fake wines used to talk about wine from 'batches.' Perhaps they knew the satire involved in their word choice, or perhaps that was just an ill-fated irony!"

No. 12 is the famed 1959 Musigny Vogue 750ml. A basic scam that has been continually put over on fine-wine consumers is the ridiculous claim that bottles have been "re-corked" or "re-conditioned." Come on, people! This is just a statement made to make the buyer forget the anomalies and accept whatever (fake) wine they get. This is a common case in which the wine has so many problems that it could not possibly, even in some strange alternate universe, be authentic.

When a wine is re-conditioned or re-corked, there should be information about what exactly happened to it in the process. Re-corked wine should have corks consistent with the original. In this case, the winery will generally state the year in which the wine was produced as well as the year in which it was re-corked. The vendor must be honest about all these issues.

If there is a recycle symbol on the capsule, but the wine is from 1951, something is wrong!

Corks are at the center of the authentication process. Other aspects of wine production can be more easily copied, but corks are ridiculously hard to get around. Most corks are insanely wrong and, unfortunately, a few fakers have been able to develop tremendous skill at counterfeiting corks. By tradition, corks have been branded. Often, there are corks that have been taken out and their vintages changed or a number scraped. Vintages can be masked with certain applications, although counterfeiters typically get so many of the features of the corks wrong that those wines can be determined to be fake and subsequently taken off the market.[46]

According to some reports, as much as 70% of wine on the Chinese market is fake wine.[47]

Bruno Paumard couldn't stop laughing as he painted a verbal picture of a fake French wine a friend gave him in 2011.[48] The bottle was white wine claiming to be from the vineyards of Romanee-Conti, the label bore the logo of Chateau Lafite-Rothschild and the supposed origin was Montpellier in the South of France.

Bruno knows, of course, that Domaine de la Romanee-Conti (known for its high quality, top vintage from Burgundy in France) makes only a miniscule amount of white wine, which is labeled Montrachet. This has nothing to do with the equally high-end Lafite from the Bordeaux region, and the brands are not produced at all near Montpellier.

Bruno called it "the most magnificent example of a hijacked brand of wine" he's ever seen. It doesn't get better than that."

Supermarkets, liquor stores, and restaurants are in a constant war against fake wine. The level of fakes

---

46 Ibid.

47 Vinography (November 8, 2013). *Almost 70% of the Wine Sold in China is Fake, Says Expert.* Available from http://www.vinography.com/archives/2013/11/almost_70_of_the_wine_sold_in.html.

48 Yue Jones, Terril (June 9, 2013). *In China, fake European wine more worrying than teriffs.* Reuters. Available from http://www.reuters.com/article/us-china-wine-fakes-idUSBRE95801Q20130609.

on the market increased as Beijing investigated wine imports coming from the European Union.

Mr. Duan Changqing, Chairman of the National Winery Committee of China, says the issue is highly convoluted, "All the wine is real," he says, "it's just the labels and the bottles are fake. So you have to be a real expert to not get fooled. When you get a fake bottle you really can't even go back to the store or collector and complain because how do you prove it? Only a handful of people in the world really have the palette developed to definitely say one way or the other, and a store clerk in downtown Beijing certainly isn't going to be one of them."

EU wine exports to China have increased more than ten-fold since 2006, a trade value of over $1 billion. The rapidly increasing wealth in China is transforming the lives and taste of the world's fastest growing major economy. No one knows what percentage of the market is cornered by copycats and fakes, according Jim Boyce who says, "Things that are faked tend to be things that are very popular."

Expensive wine is very popular in China, often more for pride than taste. Maggie Wang, who shared the wine with Nie, said, "Those expensive wines are where you see more fakes.

"But there's lots of phony wine. Everything's faked in China," she continued. "For a lot of Chinese consumers, the more expensive it is, the more they'll buy it. Chinese like things like that - they'll buy the most expensive house, drive the most expensive car. They don't want the best, they want the most expensive."

Counterfeiters focus on the European fine wines due to the high margins and high demand. The Chateau Lafite is the poster child for wine counterfeiting. A 1982 Lafite, perhaps one of the greatest vintages from the last century, may cost upwards of $10,000. For this reason, there is a powerful industry in fake Lafites in China. Wine experts say there are more cases of 1982 Lafite in China than were actually made by the chateau in that year.

Credit: Hong Kong Wine Auction

Christophe Salin, the head of Domaines Barons de Rothschild, father entity to Lafite-Rothschild, maintains that Lafite isn't the big problem. "I have never seen a bottle of fake 1982 Lafite," said Christophe, a frequent traveler to China for over 20 years. "The problem we have is the creative attitude of some Chinese. They sometimes use our name in funny ways," he said[49]. Jim Boyce added to that point by saying, "Lafite is such a generic brand in China that it has widespread appeal as a name and as a status symbol."

The mystique is greater than just the wine itself. In Beijing, there exists a "La Fite British Exoti Bar" as well as a "Beijing Lafitte Chateau Hotel." The first move for anyone who counterfeits wine is to obtain or make a bottle very much like the original. This can be hard to do. Cheng Qianrui, an editor of wine at the website Daily Vitamin, said, "People will also use real bottles with something else inside, or make labels that are spelled differently. If you know wines, you can tell, but not a lot of Chinese do."[50]

"Mouton & Sons" and "Edouard Mouton" pop up in the Chinese market a lot—fakes, says Importer Torres Wines Sales Director Sun Yu. "It happens in secondary or third-tier cities where they don't have much wine knowledge," said Sun.[51] The top winemakers are fighting back hard. They will smash wine bottles after tastings to prevent the bottles from being refilled by counterfeiters and used for resale. Major international spirits brands are taking anti-counterfeiting measures as they too fall victim to wine fraud in China. Their measures include bottle buyback programs, covert tagging of bottles, and tamper-proof caps, among others.

According to one international beverage company located in China's executive, however, these measures

---

49 Ibid.
50 Ibid.
51 Ibid.

are not as common with wine companies. Domaines Barons de Rothschild has been decorating its bottles of Chateau Lafite and Les Carruades de Lafite with tags that are "tamper-proof" ever since 2009. The elite bottles, however, have been protected since 1996, Christophe Salin, the company president, said. There are an additional four techniques for identification that he declines to reveal. "If you show me a bottle of Lafite, I can instantly tell you when it was bottled, a lot of things. To counterfeit is not easy," he said. [52] And still, why is it so prevalent in China?

New technology is on the rise to combat the forgery problem. In a few more years or less, the counterfeiting problem may be wiped out entirely. A Norwegian company is bringing us a step closer to wine bottles that can reveal their history (or something of it) to our smart phones.[53] Thinfilm unveiled "the world's first smart wine bottle." It uses a type of printed electronic tag to detect whether it has been opened and is able to wirelessly communicate this information to your smartphone. That's right! The talking wine bottle of the future is here at last!

The tag has thin electronic sensors which also have unique identifiers for wine producers to use to track bottles. The difference between this new technology and barcodes is that the information tags can't be

---

52 Ibid.

53 Munchies (July 14, 2015). *A 'Smart' Wine Bottle Could Solve China's Fake Alcohol Problem.* Available from https://munchies.vice.com/en/articles/this-smart-wine-bottle-could-solve-chinas-fake-alcohol-problem.

copied and are still readable when they're broken. It was unveiled officially at Shanghai's Mobile World Congress event and is an invention much like the "smart bottle" that Johnnie Walker released earlier in 2015. The smart bottle gives tailored messages to consumers when scanned with a smartphone. This invention may come off like an overblown method of discovering if your roommate has been taking some Pinot you were chilling in the fridge, but this tool has potentially powerful ramifications for China's fake wine market.

Russia and China are estimated to have the biggest black market for wine as well as spirits. The high demand for spirits and wine has caused a multitude of counterfeiters to fill empty bottles with industrial fake spirits and wines. With Thinfilm's printed electronic technology, wine producers could track individual bottles just as they are leaving the processing unit, making sure they are packaged, shipped, and received in their factory-sealed condition.

"Winemakers and retailers currently are in need of a cost-effective and scalable means to track and confirm the authenticity of individual wine bottles across the supply chain. This gap in the current solution set gives counterfeiters an upper hand," said Kai Leppanen, Thinfilm Chief Commercial Officer.[54]

---

54 Eads, Lauren (July 14, 2015). *Thinfilm Unveils First 'Smart' Wine Bottle*. The Drinks Business. Available from https://www.thedrinksbusiness.com/2015/07/worlds-first-smart-wine-bottle-unveiled/.

Thinfilm is currently in production on a trial version of the smart wine bottle with a Chinese owned Australian wine company. Let's look at some of the other ways wine producers can protect their brand from forgery right now.

The Chinese government and wine industry are beginning to fight back hard. The Chinese government put forth an initiative called Protected Eco-Origin Product (PEOP).[55] The government collaborates with wine producers who have joined hands with the PEOP initiative to authenticate wine by using a PEOP label. The labels have visible and invisible codes including a QR code which consumers can check with their smartphones, much like the Thinfilm technology. Most importantly, it gives people a guarantee by the government of traceability and authenticity.

Other wine producers abroad have taken the initiative to tackle the problem on their own with tamper-proof caps, bottle tagging, and barcode marking systems, among other methods. Former Australian basketball player Andrew Vlahov has developed an app for scanning wine labels to determine their authenticity. BevScan is another new technology for the determination of authenticity, developed by the Australian Wine Research Institute. It uses a beam of light that passes through the bottle without any need to open it. The light test analyzes a genuine bottle of

---

55 Park, AJ (June 4, 2015). *Cracking the Chinese wine market: part 2*. Lexology. Available from http://www.lexology.com/library/detail.aspx?g=9c4dee36-bb9d-4cd6-91f0-e4b1be8086a4.

wine and compares it to an unknown bottle. These measures are expensive and some have questions regarding their effectiveness and rightly so. There are still other, simpler proven methods for determining the authenticity of wine.

Building brand protection and awareness in China is also a critical component in the fight against fakes. When Chinese wine drinkers can easily recognize a wine company's trademarks and label features, they are more likely to bypass a fake for the real thing. Another important thing to do to protect genuine wine is to constantly monitor the Chinese wine market, especially online. Fake wines sold online are rising drastically. Websites like Ebay and Taobao should be checked regularly. When there is wine offered for sale, contact your IP advisor and they will tell you what can be done to counter a particular suspected counterfeiter.

When exporting wine to China, there is a special need to be aware of the major counterfeit issue and how you can take measures to protect yourself. Kenny Hodgart of the South China Morning Post discussed the falling market for Lafite and the rise of fake wine in general in China.[56] Kenny mentions how the prices at auction for Chateau Lafite have sunk to a ten-year low after President Xi Jinping began raising the heat on corruption. For a long time it was commonly accepted

---

56 Hodgart, Kenny (January 29, 2015). *Fake Chinese wine is as common now as Hong Kong's amusing vanity license plates.* South China Morning Post. Available from http://www.scmp.com/comment/blogs/article/1694736/fake-chinese-wine-common-now-hong-kongs-amusing-vanity-licence-plates.

wisdom to buy wine as a sound investment, even better than art or real estate, some say. While fake goods have been flooding the market in China for years, from Lamborghinis to wristwatches, those have mostly been more or less easy to detect. Detecting fake wine, however, is another matter. The best fakes have fooled serious investors, auctioneers, and even oenologists.

The level of deception is referred to as "purity" by Kenny, who says that merits awe in some respects. The scale on which this phenomenon has become widespread is astounding. The two primary ways in which this hurts the market are one: that counterfeiters decrease sales and market share for those legit producers and two: the brand strength is weakened.[57] The impact is spreading from luxury brands all the way to mid-level ones. This is a significant problem that hurts importers especially. The brand's reputation may be further diluted and damaged by the impact of the massive level of forgery.

Alcoholic beverage producers are currently adopting some of the technological methods of preventing fraud that we have mentioned. The problem with this is that once the technological solutions are adopted, the criminals' technological sophistication rapidly rises as a result. They find ways to circumvent such measures. Of course, the best solution for this is to attack the problem at its roots.

---

57 Beconcini, Paolo (February 18, 2015). *China Fake Wines – Coming Soon to a Glass Near You?* Linkedin. Available from https://www.linkedin.com/pulse/china-counterfeiters-wine-business-paolo-beconcini.

In 2012, after vociferous consumer complaints, Shanghai police raided a wine forging operation, taking over 4,000 bottles of counterfeit wine in the process. In 2013, Yantai officials found another wine forging operation and seized bottles of inexpensive Chinese wine by the thousands with foreign labels that were fake. The problem is so massive that one blogger reported 300-400 fake wines in about 100 stores.

The problem is mainly considered a "Chinese problem" that doesn't affect American wine producers, but it will not stay that way. As the profit associated with fake wine continues to increase, Chinese fakes will inevitably make their way beyond Chinese borders. Eventually, if they have not already, they will make it to shores of both America and Europe. Even with all the advanced measures currently in use against such forgery, consumer confidence and trust in a brand can still be damaged. Moreover, online vendors aid in the sales of counterfeit products, in spite of the best authentication technology. There may be a picture of a real bottle on the site, but it's not until the bottle arrives in the mail, after the wine is purchased, that the customer can determine for sure whether or not it is a counterfeit.

Wine connoisseurs must be increasingly careful in the way they make their high-end (and even mid-level purchases) for their wine collection. Unfortunately, there is no permanent solution in countering fake wine. Intelligence and an awareness of counterfeits are the best defenses for the consumer.

CHAPTER 5

THE CHATEAUS OF CHINA

ext time you plan your trip to China, you may want to add to your list of places to visit one of these incredible wine chateaus.

Hansen Winery

Chateau Hansen is a remarkable Inner Mongolian estate which has carved a huge market inside of China. It has arguably put Wuhai on the international map for wine connoisseurs.

Anthony Rose of Decanter.com took a drive from Ningxia, crossing the border into Inner Mongolia, moving through dark lands of scary-looking coalfields en route to Wuhai.[58] As he arrived at Chateau Hansen,

---

58 Rose, Anthony (May 1, 2014). *Chateau Hansen: welcome to the Gobi Desert*. Decanter. Available from http://www.decanter.com/features/chateau-hansen-welcome-to-the-gobi-desert-245923/.

he found a music band and a group of photographers awaiting his arrival. He was surrounded by local beauties wearing blue sashes as he got out of the car. Han Jiang Ping, illustrious owner, greeted Anthony with a huge smile. He shook hands with Mr. Han's director of French exports, Bruno Paumard, and other VIPs surrounding the chateau. Overhead, the explosion of fireworks was visible amid the blue sky.

Credit: Chatuea Hansen. Mr. Bruno Paumaurd, Chief Wine Maker

This is truly the kind of treatment usually reserved for visiting dignitaries and royalty. In a showy gesture, economical and pregnant with symbolism, Mr. Han unloaded a crate of perfect grapes onto a conveyor belt that came to life as the grapes landed on it. Anthony and his traveling companions were given a cup of light colored liquid. Looking like a white wine, the group discovered it was actually kumis, a traditional alcoholic beverage fermented from the milk of mares that was drunk by Genghis Khan, the great tyrant of a bygone era.

Along the edge of the border city of Wuhai, the chateau rests on the western outskirts of the Gobi Desert, near the Yellow River. Chateau Handsen makes wine and lots of it. They make two million bottles, which is a lot more than might be expected from this out of the way wine utopia in northern China mere miles from Mongolia.

Due to regular tours of the six major provincial cities, the wine is sold through the government, businesses, and retail networks to a Chinese market of 40 million people. Bruno, ex-sommelier and wine salesman with a gift for the art of the showman, has been heavily occupied with the construction of markets in the eastern cities of China and also markets abroad.

The estate is grand, European-style, verging on the grandiose, encouraging guests to retreat to its 60-bedroom luxury hotel in order to gorge themselves on local food, take trips via horseback or camel, and to visit the local art constructed of rock. The chateau receives 20,000 visitors a year.

Bruno's great aspirations are not limited by the chateau itself. The effervescent Bruno entered China in 2005 with the hope of finding a Chinese bride after becoming infatuated with Zhang Ziyi of the movie *Crouching Tiger, Hidden Dragon*. He did find a wife. He also created a publicity stunt where Chateau Hansen's 2010 Red Camel Cabernet Sauvignon was released at the aggressive price of roughly $600 a bottle.

Wuhai has existed in its present form since the 1950s. It was built via immigrant labor for the purpose of coal mining. The first grapes were planted by coal workers who grew them in their backyards. Due to the region's sand-rife soil and liberal supply of water, the grapes were supposedly rather good. In the 1990s, the local government decided to encourage private investors to introduce winemaking into the region as a way to encourage its inhabitants to move from drinking baijiu to wine.

The government supported Mr. Han's brother to start a winery, but he passed away at the young age of 50. A previous government worker who moved into the real estate sector, Mr. Han, took over the wine business. In 2001, he released his first vintage. "Initially I wasn't interested because it was a long-term investment compared with real estate. But I felt obliged to continue my brother's pioneering work and, as time wore on, I became interested in the project," Han said.[59]

Why did he become interested?

Han explained, "Wine is a healthy product with ecological benefits, and there is much culture involved in wine compared with spirits."

Chateau Hansen is now one of four wineries in the region. It is a region with unique conditions for growing grapes. Being in Northern China and 1,500 meters above sea level, Wuhai has tremendous advantages in its dry climate, abundance of sunshine,

---

59 Ibid.

and sandy earth. The winters are bitterly cold, however, causing the necessity of vines to be buried each year in order to protect them. The bounteous water supply of the Yellow River is what nurtures the grapes, as it flows east from the Tibetan Plateau to Shandong.

Having little pollution and not too many pests or diseases has allowed Chateau Hansen to obtain China's AA organic certification (in 2007). The chateau produces 70 different wines from 370 hectares. It owns 200 hectares in three locations: in Ningxia; in a windy region 60 kilometers away where a massive, underground water supply was discovered and is now drawn upon via channels built by the winery coming from the Yellow River; and locally.

The remainder of the grape supply comes from local growers controlled by Hansen, and also growers in two neighboring provinces in Ningxia; one to the south, and one in Gansu to the west. The yields are low (Bruno says they are too low) and this is the factor, perhaps more pronounced than any other, that helps produce red wine and, more recently, white (Chardonnay, Riesling, and Semillon) of great interest and concentration.

Originally, indigenous grapes were planted because of their ability to survive harsh winter conditions. Lately, the chateau has planted Cabernet Sauvignon and Merlot along with the local grape, the Cabernet Gernischt. Cabernet Gernischt is vigorous, though not very fertile, and well-equipped to thrive in sandy soils.

It displays the varietal's well-known herbal, capsicum character.

Though great winemaking challenges still remain in the region, the primary challenge lies in teaching local growers to respect the quality and health of the vine, how to determine what the best vines for the area are, and last but not least, figuring out how to deal with the harsh winters that threaten the extinction of the vines.

From Hansen's extensive cellars, Anthony and his crew tasted a well-made Chardonnay, a Hong Se Pu Cabernet that tasted much like Margaret River, a decadently spicy Wuhai Cabernet, and a rich Ninxia Cabernet Sauvignon with a very cassis-like flavor. Tasting from the bottle, the Wuhai Valley Caberet Gernischt has a peppery Carmenere flavor. A great, unoaked red, it is one of Hansen's best wines for the price.

The Red Camel Cabernet Sauvignon of Ningxia proved to be one of Anthony's favorites. He called it, "powerful with sweet prune and plum fruit, even chocolate, deliberately made in an Amarone-style with a portion of late-harvest grapes." He did not, however, find it to be worth the $600. He thought $60 was closer to what it should be priced. He also liked Hansen's Rimage de Cabernet Gernischt, Vallée de Wuhai 2010, calling it "quirky" and "boasting aromas of Lapsang Souchong, licorice, and blueberry."

Credit: Chatuea Hansen. Mr. Bruno Paumaurd, Chief Wine Maker

As Anthony and his entourage were leaving, Mr. Han told them that the local government announced a support pack of $150 million over the next 10 years in order to establish 7,000 hectares of vineyards of the organic variety. Chateau Hansen is tremendously successful already considering its tourism business and its local market in which the wines command an average price of $15 per bottle. With the help of the government's investment, Mr. Han is poised to take a high position in the international wine market. These are truly exciting times for the remarkable Chateau Hansen.[60]

Helan Qingxue Winery

Helan Qingxue is one of the vineyards of northwestern China's Ningxia region, which have made China one of the world's top five wine producers. For those believers in the poetics of the vine, there is an interesting footnote in the region's history. Ningxia's famous Helan Mountain once inspired a Ming Dynasty controller to pen a verse called "Helan Qingxue," which is where the winery gets its name.

Helan Qingxue is co-owned by Zhang Jing, a bespectacled, young wine enthusiast who is fast establishing herself as a force to be reckoned with in the world of Chinese wine. Her soft voice and sweet

---

60 Moran, Tracy (June 7, 2014). *Meet China's Wine Whisperer: Zhang Jing*. USA Today. Available from http://www.usatoday.com/story/money/business/2014/06/07/ozy-china-wine-whisperer/10071707/.

manner make it easy to mistake her for a kid, but the truth is this 37-year-old mother is a well-educated, highly trained wine aficionado who has devoted her life to fermented grapes. Jing is the child of provincial government employees who grew up an hour by car from the vineyard.

Credit: Helan Qingxue winery, Mrs. Zhang Jing, founder

Jing's first taste of wine was in Beijing. "I fell in love with wine. From that moment, I knew I found what I wanted to do my whole life," said Jing.

In the Shanxi province, she earned her master's and bachelor's degrees before heading to Rhone Valley in France for wine training. She worked a stint at one vineyard in Australia and then collaborated with a wine producer in South Africa. From 2005, marking the opening of the Chateau Helan Qingxue, she worked for a decade at perfecting vintages and varieties of grapes. News of her finely honed abilities is now spreading fast.

Congratulating her on the birth of her daughter in 2009, a friend gave Jing five French oak barrels. What came out of those five barrels? A baby by the name of Jia Bei Lan, or "Little Feet." Jing had her daughter's tiny footprints printed on the barrels for luck and used them for the storage of vintage wine.

In 2011, the wine was awarded the title of Best Bordeaux in its class – and Jing the first Chinese winemaker to attain the prestigious honor. The wine was a dry Cabernet Sauvignon, Merlot, and Cabernet Gernicht mix.

The appearance of Jing's vineyard may be somewhat Spartan but she makes no bones about it. She said, "There are no grand buildings or luxurious decoration." As is common with boutique wineries, hers has a small production in the range of 50,000 bottles per year. In comparison, Gallo, the largest producer in the world, boasts almost 900 million bottles annually.

Helan Qingxue cultivates Cabernet Sauvignon, Merlot, Chardonnay, and Cabernet Gernischt. At 37 acres of vines, the winery has revenue in the hundreds of thousands of dollars per year. While that number is steadily increasing, Jing is not really interested in it. What she is interested in is quality over quantity. This is a good sign not only for her boutique winery, but for the quality of wine in China in general.

If you ask her what's different about her process, Jing will bring your attention to her grapevines, which are wide enough so that they can be rotated and buried in the winter in order to protect them from the harsh cold. Jing says that it is key to respect the soil in order to attain success. She adds that her wine reflects the spirit of the local terrior. In doing so, the Jia Bei Lan delivers a "fresh fruity nose, mint, plum, fresh black currant aromas, and a hint of vanilla and smoke."

Credit: Helan Qingxue winery, Mrs. Zhang Jing, founder

"If you want to go into the wine industry, you must make a long-term plan, not be anxious for success," Jing said. Every good vineyard starts with great grapes, and this requires patience – and hers is paying off. In 2013 at the Chinese RVF wine awards, she was given the name of Winemaker of the Year, which are annual recognitions given out by the Chinese version of the French magazine La Revue du Vin de France. She also garnered recognition as the Outstanding Winemaker of China in the Fine Wine Challenge. Jancis Robinson of the Financial Times named Jing a "gifted winemaker." In addition, Chateau Helan Qingxue, along with just five other vineyards, was included in the Map for World Wine Regions. This was the first time the wineries in Ningxia's Helan Mountains were included.

In the not too distant past, Chinese wine was not much more than fermented grape juice with extra sugar. Now, of course, that has all changed and the Chinese palate is becoming much more sophisticated. Furthermore, the recent surge in wine consumption in China has been noticed by foreign investors. New wineries made possible by foreign investment are being built across China. Jing remains optimistic, though she admits China's wine industry is still seeing its early days. She works hard to ensure that, one day perhaps, her daughter will be able to taste her mother's fine wine on the tables of foreign countries.

Chateau Changyu Moser XV

The Chateau Changyu Moser XV is perhaps the grandest chateau in China, located in Yinchuan, the capital of the autonomous province of Ningxia. It was developed in collaboration with Lenz Moser of the famous Austrian wine family.[61]

It officially opened for business in August 2013. The French-style chateau is a Disney-like experience in the Chinese wine world. The 150-acre estate serves as local headquarters to Changyu Pioneer Wine. The winery features an 800-barrel wine cellar and a high-tech bottling line. Every stage of the wine production takes place within the chateau including viticulture, pressing, fermentation, maturation, and bottling. There is also a museum inside the chateau dedicated to the history of Changyu and of Chinese winemaking.

A long and welcoming string of flowing fountains connects the main building with the estate entrance. Many couples choose this lovely venue for Western-style castle weddings or wedding photo sessions. The imagery of the French-style chateau surrounded by water and the vast surrounding vineyard exudes an aura of romance.

The 200-meter skywalk is one of the best ways to appreciate Changyu. The skywalk showcases the rich history, the chateau's layout, and its outstanding wine products. On a trek through the world's longest wine-themed gallery, visitors are taken back in time while viewing wine history, art, and culture.

---

61 http://www.changyu.com.cn:8189/content/details15_3220.html

At the end of the gallery there is a Dome Cinema that is the first of its kind in northwest China. Visitors can experience a wine-themed movie, which includes music composed by a famous Chinese musician and performed by the Asian Philharmonic Orchestra. After the movie, visitors can enter the mesmerizing lobby and experience wine-themed murals painted on arched ceilings.

Visitors can also view the wine bottling through a massive glass window which includes bottle washing, filling, corking, and labeling. The underground wine cellar is the largest in Ningxia with wine being aged in more than 800 oak barrels. The temperature of the cellar is kept between 14-16 degrees Celsius throughout the year and the humidity is maintained between 70% and 80%. Indeed, this wine cellar is truly splendid and wine lovers can even store their favorite wine there for a fee.

The second floor of the wine museum depicts how the chateau's name was derived. It is named after the chateau's Chief Winemaker, Laurenz Moser, descendant of the famous Austrian Lenz Moser wine family. The Moser family represents five generations of winemaking experience where the legendary Professor Lorenz Moser III earned international fame for his invention of the Austrian trellising system, which revolutionized vineyard cultivation across Europe.

Chateau Changyu Moser XV is also the name of the estate's flagship wine, which is a blend of 85% cabernet sauvignon, 10% merlot and 5% Syrah. The chateau's second wine, named Moser Family, is a single varietal cabernet sauvignon.

Chateau Changyu Moser XV is known for providing an amazing wine tour experience. Whether you have an appreciation for wine history, European decadence and photography, or want to embrace wine culture at another level, this spectacular chateau in Ningxia offers something for everyone.[62]

---

62 Ibid.

CONCLUSION

From the streets of New York's Chinatown to Helan Qingxue at the foothills of the Helan Mountains in China, never would I have imagined sipping my way around the world and telling the untold stories of the Chinese wine industry. Combining my heritage and passion for wine, I've become enthralled by Chinese wine producers who have gone from selling low grade wines to producing quality wines that are now winning medals. Their stories are the ones this industry is built on and will boost it to thrive.

Dating back to 1892, Changyu Pioneer Wine was one of the first wineries to be established in China. Located in Yantai - a coastal city in the province of Shandong - this area is still the country's largest producer of wine today. Historically, winemaking was among the first industries that saw domestic and foreign investors join forces in China. Today, wineries such as Helan Qingxue are quickly becoming leaders in the Chinese wine industry, and repeating history as domestic and foreign forces join in economic reform.

The early involvement and investment of major French brands in 1979 has not only grown the Chinese wine industry, but also produced the "Big Three" of Chinese wine - Changyu, Great Wall, and Dynasty. These three wineries, which are recognized as producing quality wines, now own the majority of wine vineyards in the country with a combined estimated revenue of $8 billion.

The involvement of French wine brands in the local Chinese market has generated consumer interest in domestic wines. With affluent Chinese consumers being highly brand conscious, the growing appetite of indulgent wines has similarly centered on prestigious names including the French imported Rothschild. Because of Rothschild's popularity in China, the company started its own 37-acre Chinese vineyard in 2011 signaling a strong belief in the growing wine industry in China.

Stemming from the economic development and rise of the middle class, China is currently the world's largest wine market. Many of China's wineries have been focusing on producing quality wine and have resulted in favorable ratings from international wine critics. I believe that in a few years Chinese wines will be available at fine restaurants in New York and London, which is almost unheard of today. At one time, Chile, California, and South Africa had up-and-coming wine industries that were churning out low grade wines. After years of hard work that included marketing, education and setting up the proper distribution channels, wines from all these regions are now receiving accolades. The current success of these wine regions gives hope that China will follow in a similar way.

Today, Chinese wine can be found on the menus of high-end restaurants and hotels in Shanghai, and are being reviewed by top wine critics from around the world. Unfortunately, that is where it ends. Outside of China, it is still very difficult to find good Chinese wine, as most of China's high-end wineries are currently producing their wines on a small scale, which does not give them the ability to compete with Australian, European, and American competitors.

The Chinese wine industry still has a long way to mature. With the exception of Hong Kong and Macau, there is still a huge untapped market in China's vast population and therefore there is no rush to sell abroad. However, the rapidly growing middle class has opened up an amazing opportunity for winemakers in China to thrive in the domestic market. In the next few years, the Chinese wine industry will continue to evolve and one day may show the world incredible wines that even the toughest critics would praise and enjoy.

CITATIONS

https://www.nzte.govt.nz/en/export/market-research/wine/ wine-in-china/

http://www.winespectator.com/webfeature/show/id/52194 http://www.winesandvines.com/template.cfm?section=features&content=95708

http://www.wine-searcher.com/m/2013/06/top-12-wine-fakes

http://www.decanter.com/features/chateau-hansen-welcome-to-the-gobi-desert-245923/

http://www.usatoday.com/story/money/business/2014/06/07/ozy-china-wine-whisperer/10071707/

http://www.vinography.com/archives/2013/11/almost_70_of_the_wine_sold_in.html

http://www.reuters.com/article/us-china-wine-fakes-idUSBRE95801Q20130609

http://munchies.vice.com/articles/this-smart-wine-bottle-could-solve-chinas-fake-alcohol-problem

http://www.lexology.com/library/detail.aspx?g=9c4dee36-bb9d-4cd6-91f0-e4b1be8086a4

http://www.scmp.com/comment/blogs/article/1694736/fake-chinese-wine-common-now-hong-kongs-amusing-vanity-licence-plates

https://www.linkedin.com/pulse/china-counterfeiters-wine-business-paolo-beconcini

http://www.changyu.com.cn:8189/content/details15_3220.html

http://www.telegraphindia.com/pressrelease/prnw/en53110.html#.Vr5BQbQrJkg

http://www.forbes.com/sites/niallmccarthy/2015/04/29/china-surpasses-france-in-vineyards-but-trails-in-wine-production-infographic/#637810ab6375

https://www.sciencedaily.com/releases/2015/05/150506095142.htm

http://beveragetradenetwork.com/en/btn-academy/articles/china-uncovered-interview-with-one-of-the-largest-wine-importers-in-china-330.htm

China

www.ingramcontent.com/pod-product-compliance
Lightning Source LLC
Chambersburg PA
CBHW052056070526
44584CB00017B/2201